STEPHEN A. BLY

Quality Living

IN A COMPLICATED AGE

HERE'S LIFE PUBLISHERS, INC.
San Bernardino, California 92402

QUALITY LIVING IN A COMPLICATED AGE
by Stephen A. Bly

Published by
HERE'S LIFE PUBLISHERS, INC.
P.O. Box 1576

ISBN 0-89840-071-6
Library of Congress Catalog Number 84-47803
HLP Product Number 950808

Scripture quotations are from:
The Living Bible
©Tyndale House Publishers 1971
The New American Standard Bible
©The Lockman Foundation 1960, 1962, 1963, 1968,
    1971, 1972, 1973, 1975, and are used by permission.

Selected other books by Stephen A. Bly:
RADICAL DISCIPLESHIP, Moody Press, 1981
GOD'S ANGRY SIDE, Moody Press, 1982

TO: John, Pat, Dave, Cindy, Wally, Heather, Alan, Gae, Joe, Brad, Tom, Judy, Lindy, Shel, Sam, Caroline, Sheila, Lois, Paul, Tracy, Russ, Cathy, Brian, Jesse, Bill, Karen, Debbie, Tim, Missy, Joy ... and all the others at Ron's Place.

Contents

CHAPTER 1
How To Get The Best Out Of Life

CHAPTER 2
Who Will Remember Me At The Class Reunion?

CHAPTER 3
Will They Ever Stop Calling Me Junior?

CHAPTER 4
I'd Like To Stop Asking,
"How Much Does It Cost?"

CHAPTER 5
I've Got To Find A Job That Doesn't
Bore Me To Tears

CHAPTER 6
Why Watch Television Alone?

CHAPTER 7
Sure I Care About What I Eat—
But Not Very Much!

CHAPTER 8
The Big Plunge

CHAPTER 9
Is There Life Without Panic?

CHAPTER 10
What If The Elevator Cable Snaps?

CHAPTER 11
Is It Really Worth Getting Up
Early On Sundays?

CHAPTER 12
Come On Along!

CHAPTER 1
HOW TO GET THE BEST OUT OF LIFE

No escape.

They are all around us.

The bookstore is full of them.

Coffee tables across America strain under their weight.

You are not safe even at the supermarket. Right where you would least expect it—between the instant potatoes and frozen pizza—everywhere—books, articles, and posters proclaim the Age of Austerity.

"Life With Limits"

"More With Less"

"More With Even Lesser"

I you believe everything you read, you might conclude that the good times have passed you by. *The Wall Street Journal* stated that young people " ... are under unusually severe stress these days brought on by a cross-current of unusually poor job prospects, weakening family support and a bewildering array of choices" (*The Wall Street Journal*, June 1, 1983). All the abundance, the fun, the first-class experience have vanished, all used up by a generation you just missed.

Don't believe it.

Sure, gas prices are four times higher than ten

years ago, but new cars get three times better mileage.

Jobs are tight. No one will argue that. But there are still some wide open fields.

It takes an oil well to buy a new house, but there is a growing market of creative alternatives.

No doubt about it, there are limitations. However, that does not mean we have to be satisfied with junk. Quantity may have to be reduced, but not quality. Times are tough for many. You might not have everything you want now. But why not aim for first rate, instead of being satisfied with second best?

I call it quality living in a complicated age. A great way to live. A goal to achieve. You can begin to taste it today. It is an exhilarating existence, and I wouldn't settle for anything less.

Of course, there are some obstacles.

FIRST OBSTACLE: COMPLEXITY OF LIFE

The simple, rural, slow-pace existence in which the average person is given days and months to make decisions will elude most of us. We live on the run: run to school, run to work, run through dinner, run across town, run to the concert, collapse in bed, then rise early for a jog. We are always a step behind, and find that some good things in life burst just as we grasp them.

It is the Age of Computers, the pundits explain. Who can argue? A recent magazine article explained that you should begin to teach your children about the wonderful world of bytes and discs at age three; only the kids will be able to keep up with the fast-moving computer industry. Stay away from the scene for six months, and you'll never get back in—so they say.

Molly is only twenty-seven. She still lives in her small central California home town. When she was growing up, it was so safe the doors were never locked. The keys stayed in the car overnight. A stranger at the door received a sandwich, cookies and a glass of milk. Now, the same house has deadbolts on the doors, iron bars across the kitchen windows, and an ear-piercing siren hooked up to the entrances. A stranger at the door means, call the police.

Jodi made up her mind at the age of fourteen what she wanted to do with her life. There was no changing her mind. She knew she needed four years of college and three more of grad school, but it would be worth it, she explained. It wasn't. Oh, she made it through all right. But now she's thirty, a success in her field, and bored to tears.

Mark enjoyed going to church as a kid. He liked the songs. He liked the thought that there was Someone worth sitting still for. He liked to play kick-the-can at the youth activities. But, by the time his professors bombarded him with their demythological, existential, anthropomorphical theology, he realized he suffered from a religious complexity overload.

SECOND OBSTACLE: DOUBT

Lots of folks just don't believe that quality living is obtainable.

Now, it is true that I don't know your particular circumstances. I have no idea how rough it is where you sit. Your financial and social pressures are unknown to me. You may be tapped out spiritually. But I do know that doubt slows down your pursuit of the good life, wherever you are.

7

Lynn planned to spend the summer on a leisure tour of Europe. It was to be her graduation present to herself. Then someone ran into her parked car and it was totaled. She took a job, and postponed the trip for a year. Then there was the surgery on her foot. That was five years ago. She has been transferred [across the country] by her company, and she lost half her belongings to a burglar. Besides, the company won't let her off for a three-month vacation until she has worked twenty-five years. "I'll never spend a summer in Europe!" she moans. She may be right.

This book doesn't promise you the moon, but it does offer a piece of moon rock that will be grade A. The times in which we live might shoot down some of our dreams, but what we have left can be pure gold. Quality living is within anyone's reach. No kidding. No doubts.

THIRD OBSTACLE: GUILT

Tell everyone about the condo you are saving for and you'll hear cries of "You're out of step with the real world." Or, "What about the starving refugees?" And "Why bother, we'll all be blown up, anyway."

Bart loves to ski. When he had an opportunity to work in Colorado he jumped at the chance. Then his sister called. In no uncertain terms she told him how inconsiderate he would be to move so far away from the family. Now Bart has a choice. He can stay, with many regrets, or move to Colorado under a load of guilt.

Too often when we reach a goal in the search for quality living someone dumps a guilt trip on us. At times they have a valid point, but many times they don't. They don't really believe it themselves, or live it. Less competition, that is what they are after.

But quality living, without guilt, can be had.

FOURTH OBSTACLE: AIMLESSNESS

Contentment with hopes and wishes, rather than plans and actions, are enemies of quality living. Aimlessness can strike our relationships. That is why many of them "go nowhere." It plagues our vocations, drumming good workers into boredom. Aimlessness strikes at material goals as well.

Carl dreamed for years of owning a sports car. Dreams are free, but they don't accomplish much. Carl owed a bundle on his little import, and with no ready cash, he felt doomed to a four-cylinder future.

So he developed a plan. He figured that if he used public transportation he could sell his present car and get $1,000 for his equity. He could then bank the $200-per-month car payments. That would total $3,400 the first year, plus interest.

The Mini-Mart around the corner offered him a weekend job. After deductions, he would clear another $300 per month. That would make $7,000 at the end of the first year, $13,000 after two, with the interest covering his bus tokens. His dream car is only two years away. Carl has a plan.

FIFTH OBSTACLE: HALF-HEARTEDNESS

If it doesn't come easily, as by Uncle Harry leaving us his millions, most of us quit too soon or never even try. In his novel *First Circle* (New York: Harper and Row, 1968) Aleksandr Solzhenitsyn states that too many people bring projects to a 99% completion. They never find either perfection or satisfaction. Quality achievement requires pushing out to Solzhenit-syn's "final inch."

Every morning before class Jeanie jogs across campus, down Beck Country Road to the seventh oak tree, and back to the house. It is a four-mile course. She is tempted to stop by each of the oaks, saying, "It wouldn't hurt to turn around now. No one is watching." Or, "Maybe I counted wrong." Sometimes she gives in and cuts the course short. She can always feel the difference. Three and a half miles may be a good workout for others, but it is not quality for Jeanie.

SIXTH OBSTACLE: A FAULTY LIFESCOPE

Some aim for quality in only one area of their lives. In finances. Or a vocation. Maybe in a relationship. But true quality involves the total scope of your life. A long-range planner will push to excellence in every direction possible. That is why this book's content is so diverse.

What will quality living be for you? It is hard to say. But let me tell you how the idea has shaped my life. Maybe you will get some ideas.

I live out west. Always have. I happen to be fond of western paintings. Charlie Russell is my favorite. I would love to have an original, but the cost is out of my league.

I've found two alternatives. A museum in West Yellowstone sells Russell prints reproduced on canvas. Adding a frame keeps the cost within reason. Not an original, but it is not a magazine decoupage either.

Or if I want an original painting, I can go see a fellow who lives up the Yankee Fork. He paints in Russell's style, and for me that is quality.

I have traveled from northern Idaho to southern California. A time or two I've been camping in the rain when a deluxe travel home pulls up beside me. I must admit a twinge of envy. My soaked tent feels colder than ever.

However, I prefer what to me is a quality vacation. Last week I drove my old four-wheel drive down a winding road to the bottom of the deepest gorge in North America. The Snake River cuts a path 7,000 feet below the mountain peaks, in Hell's Canyon. I hiked along the river and stared up at heights that easily would dwarf the Sears Tower in Chicago. My cost? One dollar to camp, and a little gas money. The view of the deer, elk, and eagles also came at the same low price. A travel home never would have made it down and back. That is what I call quality.

Recently, I made a trip to central California to see Mom. I had only a few hours to spare and wanted to do three things. First, we drove to town for Chinese food, her favorite and mine. We had time to talk and she took a break from the kitchen. Second, I spent the evening fixing a kitchen appliance, and third, the next morning I repaired her backyard sprinkler system.

A six-hour trip to fix some sprinklers?

You see, Dad died a few years ago. I am her only son. She doesn't nag; I just look for these projects. Those little odd jobs are reminders that there is still a son who cares. This is part of quality family life for me.

I bought a house located in northern Idaho. At 4,000 feet the pines, firs, and spruce in the woods across the road lap onto our place. On sunny days you can see through the trees to the sparkling lake beyond. The air is bright and clean. The sky is pure blue. The snow is a glimmering white.

How did I do it? I aimed for it. It took years, but it's what I wanted. Quality.

For months I crammed a couple dozen high school kids into the living room of that Idaho home. We would laugh, play, read, study, and sometimes cry together. They would tell me about their dates, describe their basketball plays, complain about English exams, and wonder why they couldn't communicate with their parents.

Some people seemed amazed that I was so eager to have them back week after week. They didn't realize how much those kids meant to me. I need to do more than just survive. I have a need to touch others. I have a desire to have a good effect on my world, however small or large it may be. I want to know that I'm leaving behind a positive influence. So, I shared my knowledge of God and my personal faith in Jesus Christ with these kids. Keeping the door of my home open is part of my striving for a quality lifescope.

In my personal search for a quality lifescope, I've discovered five principles.

1. A quality lifescope must include the body, mind, soul and spirit.

You can stuff your garage, and even your brain, with quality, but if you ignore your soul and spirit, you will still find yourself empty.

Terri and Jeannette grew up together. They shared classes from the fourth grade through high school. Then Jeannette was killed in a car accident. Terri attended the funeral. As she stood by the grave, she wept, more for herself than Jeannette.

"It could have been me. Is that how life is meant

to end? A polished wooden casket lowered into a dark, muddy hole? Is that all there is?"

Was Jeannette only a physical organism that had now disappeared as though she had never existed? The thought plagued Terri.

Those who live only for gratification of the body's comfort will starve their soul and spirit. It takes more than pleasure and education to produce deep contentment.

Cut off my legs or give me a heart transplant, I'm still me. I'm no less a person, unless my spirit gives up. The spirit doesn't show up in an x-ray, but it's there. It's the part of me that makes me who I am. A lifescope that ignores the spirit will always be dwarfed.

2. Quality living cannot be achieved at the expense of others.

Hoping others fail so you may succeed is hardly quality.

Gary and Lance began to work at the fast food chain during their sophomore year. The pay was minimal, but it was a job. By their senior year, they were leading contenders for assistant manager's position. It meant a pay hike, an opportunity to pay off those school loans. No one could guess who would get the position.

Then, rumors began to filter to the manager about Lance. Some talk about unethical procedures, some dishonesties. The rumors in time proved to be false, but the job was given to Gary, who had started the rumors. Maybe that was good enough for him, but not for me. I want my quality place in life to be secured fair and square.

3. Quality living is not easy.

Hard work, going against the current, and sacrifice are the normal path. Some folks misunderstand. Often you will ask yourself, is it worth it? Personal discipline, integrity, and singleness of purpose require constant effort.

It was inspiring. The harmony between music, ice, and body thrilled the audience. Trinka is a great figure skater—so smooth, fluid, relaxed. She is aiming for the Olympics. She has a fifty-fifty chance of making it. Ask her what all this is costing her and she will reply quickly, "A sixth of my life. Four hours every day, seven days a week, fifty-two weeks a year, ever since I was eight years old."

It is worth it to her, even if there is only a fifty percent chance of qualifying. Is there anything you consider worth giving up a sixth of your life for? Quality often costs that much, and more.

4. *Quality living often produces surprises.*

Derrick contemplated skipping Poly Sci that day. Finals would soon be here and a trip to the library seemed more profitable than a less-than-stirring, but important, lecture. At the last moment, though, he opted for the Poly Sci class.

"Does anyone want a summer job?" the prof asked. "There is a candidate for state office who needs someone to serve on his campaign staff."

Derrick volunteered. So did others. He got the job, and for several years he whirled through the action of California politics. A spur-of-the-moment decision provided years of quality living.

You will need to watch for unexpected opportunities that lead to excellence.

5. *Do not settle for anything less.*

Do you want to live at the beach? Don't settle for a wall-size photograph of the waves. Do you want to lose ten pounds? Then seven won't do. Want a doctorate? Why quit after a master's? Do you want a quality spiritual life? Don't settle for a cheap imitation. Coach class is better than economy, but it is a long way from first class. The same is true of quality living in a complicated age.

Is it just a mirage?

Perhaps for some.

But not for me. Or you!

Chapter 2
Who Will Remember Me
At The Class Reunion?

She chatted with me as we stood in line. She mentioned an art institute in Paris, a home in Colorado, a hybrid rose named after her, and a book project that required most of her time. She interspersed old memories of our alma mater. Cynthia had come a long way since being president of the French club and flautist in the Redwood High School Ranger Marching Band.

We stopped at the desk for our registration cards. An old high school photo adorned each corner. She stared at mine. "You were in our class?" she asked.

"Of course, what else?"

"Oh, I just assumed you were someone's guest." She smiled with a slight blush. "Isn't it funny how you can spend four years in a school this size and never getting around to meeting everyone?"

I nodded, and strolled to the punch bowl. I resisted the impluse to run back to her and say, "Good grief, Cynthia, we sat next to each other all four years in English!" My pride wouldn't let me.

Nothing like a reunion to get reacquainted with close friends!

You can survive without friends, of course. People isolate themselves in caves, on islands, or within urban hideouts. You can get along somehow this way, but it is not quality. Nothing is more satisfying than a good give-and-take with a fellow human, or so depressing as a friendship that fails.

Crisp blue air. White puffies. A light breeze rolling in from puget sound. Beautiful Seattle. Amy stood right where she wanted to be. She was beginning her junior year of college. Though she was 1,200 miles away from home, her dream was coming true. Of course, she had no friends here, yet. No big deal. She was sure she would grow close to her roommate, Suzi.

Wrong. Suzi moved out at the semester break. Then came Meg. She didn't last 'til Easter. Never heard from her again.

WHY DON'T FRIENDSHIPS LAST?

One reason is, we don't work at it. Remember how hard you tried to establish a relationship with that certain someone? Maybe you drove around the block a dozen times so that you might pass her just once on the sidewalk. Or, when you nursed your medium coke for three hours, just in case the right fellow might find you there. Or, how you tensed your muscles in rugged determination for those extra excruciating minutes in order to be in top form should the VIP happen to storm through the gym door.

We often work to began relationships. We don't always work to keep them going.

Sometimes we are complacent. "But, we always play racquetball on Thursdays!" Sometimes we are ignorant. "I just assumed everything was okay!" Sometimes we are too tired. "I just need to be by myself. I thought you would understand."

When Amy and Suzi greeted each other that first

night in September, they talked until 3 A.M. A synopsis of their life stories, detailed descriptions of boyfriends, adventures experienced, and dreams for the future. The session ended in tears, though, when Suzi admitted her lifelong struggle with being overweight.

Amy determined to help Suzi reach her personal goal. Week after week they tried one diet after another. No progress. Every conversation included mention of Suzi's battle. Every day closed with the particulars of that day's menu and exercise schedule. Finally, Amy couldn't take it any more. She blew up.

"Suzi, I'm tired of talking about your weight! You could slim down if you really stuck to something. Be consistent with something, anything. Meanwhile, keep quiet about it, I just don't want to hear it."

Communication almost ceased after that. Social times together diminished. Amy felt isolated. Suzi soon moved.

Suzi has a problem. That is obvious. But so does Amy. She doesn't know how to build a lasting friendship. Her problem may be more serious than Suzi's, because she doesn't recognize it yet.

Friendships fail when we set narrow requirements. We all thrill to find others who think just as we do. We need the agreement, the affirmation of our general philosophy of life. We assume such people will be just like we are in every way. No one is.

Ken and Michelle both labored at the evening shift of the local fast food resturant. As the walks home extended to freguent dates, the other workers sensed a serious commitment. They were all shocked when Ken suddenly stopped talking to Michelle and asked to be transferred to another shift. The story finally drifted to the surface.

One night at Ken's house, he demonstrated the finer points of his expensive stereo. He included a tour of his album collection, which was a floor-to-ceiling wall display and a copy of every #1 ranked rock hit since 1962.

"Well, what do you think?" Ken prodded

"It's impressive, all right," Michelle countered as she sorted through the racks.

"Any particular song you want to hear?" he pressed.

"You got any Barbara Mandrell?"

"What?"

"How about Willie? Or Waylon? Maybe a Gilly or a Milsap or even the Stats?"

"Your putting me on...aren't you?"

"Surely you have a Tanya Tucker or Lacy J. Dalton? How about Kenny Rogers, or Glen Campbell?"

"Come on, that stuff's not even music,"

"Not even John Denver?"

Ken fumed in disbelief. He firmly led Michelle out of his sacred room, and after an awkward hour of trying to regain the old, easy banter, he drove her home. She had not met his requirements.

We do need limits. Some behavior is unpleasant to be around. Some language used grates our ears. Some actions harm our minds and bodies. But, it is possible to be so confining that we really don't get along with anyone other than ourselves (and sometimes there is tension there too).

Friendships falter when we avoid taking personal risks. Relationships cannot deepen unless we talk about deep subjects, unless we open up a bit of ourselves to public view.

There are good reasons for remaining tight-lipped. Betrayal hurts. Such painful experiences may require years of being tenderly nursed back to health. Our environment may also smother our abilty to give more than the superficial niceties. Demands of perfectionist parents still may choke attempts to admit struggle, no matter how long it has been since you left the nest.

During times of wrestling with self-image, we tend to keep people at a distance, fearful of what they will find if they get too close.

Suzi's battle with the bulge was more than just a problem to tackle. It consumed her. This obstacle tripped her emotional and social, as well as her physical, balance. Amy didn't understand. For one thing, she had never had a weight problem. She had trouble admitting any real problems at all.

She had a cozy philosophy: "If you don't admit, to yourself or others, that you have a weakness, then you don't."

This was her protection, her guard and defense against life. A feeble foundation, perhaps, but she had sailed along pretty well with it, so far.

How do you know when you need to risk opening yourself up to another person? Here are a few examples—

When you've tried for years to work through a problem, and you are about to go under.

When your potential friend has been receiving a lopsided view of who you really are. That friend may need to see your Clark Kent side, as well as your ability to leap tall buildings.

When another person's warfare is in an arena in which you've had firsthand experience.

20

When your inner struggles dictate the direction in which the relationship is moving.

When your life's confused with a complexity overload.

Another reason some fledgling friendships fail is that we try to imitate other people's patterns. Who sets your example of how friendships ought to be? Laverne and Shirley? Tom Selleck? Norman Mailer? Tennessee Williams? General Hospital? The National Enquirer? Your older brother? Your parents? Your co-workers? Who is it?

You might not be Butch Cassidy to the Sundance Kid, or Han Solo to Luke Skywalker, but you can make good friends. You are unique, and worth knowing. Your potential friend is one of a kind, and worth knowing. Therefore, your combined relationship will be unlike any other.

Some friendships crack because of the unsolved problems of one of the participants. Amy wearied of Suzi's incessant dwelling in the pit of despair.

Check yourself out. Do the same topics dominate your every conversation? The most common topics might be your:

1. physical condition—including looks, health, weight;
2. relationships—family, professors/bosses, the opposite sex;
3. mistreatment—how you have been cheated, slandered, and taken advantage of.

Close friends should be able to share these things with us, but they also need relief from the same old complaints. You should be making progress, getting somewhere with eliminating some of the morass of negative information.

A final reason some friendships are broken is the

strain of the forced versus the natural. Remember when you were a kid and Mom dragged you along to the Garden Club leader's meeting and you had to play with Chuckie Robinson? Your mother was delighted that you had a playmate. She didn't realize that dear Chuckie shot rubber darts at you, stomped on your Lego buildings, and liked to bite. And Mom insisted on inviting Chuckie to your birthday party and to other special events. "After all," she reminded you, ignoring your glare, "Chuckie's Mom and I ... "

Now, we force ourselves into unnatural friendships. It goes like this.

The first day on the job you are introduced to your new supervisor. He is new, but looks like a winner, a future executive type. You decide it will be to your best advantage to get to know him better. You discover he likes tennis. You drop a few hints about your own tennis ability, ask him for a recommendation for re-stringing your racquet, and discuss with him the next probable Wimbledon winner.

The truth is, you have not played since freshman P.E. You barely escape humiliation on the court by twisting your ankle in the second set.

Next, you try eating lunch at the same place, parking next to his car, and wearing the same brand suit. This is not the same as working at a friendship. There needs to be as much sensitivity to the other person's needs, as there is to his usefulness.

THERE ARE LEVELS OF FRIENDSHIP

It helps to remember that all friendships are not created equal.

FIRST—THOSE ON YOUR SIDE OF THE LINE.

Did you ever draw a line in the dirt and challenge

those on your side to cross over? We do it mentally all the time, sifting our friendships out from the multitude. We divide our world into categories such as,

Democrats ... Republicans
aggies ... skinheads
joggers ... iron men
Dodgers ... Yankees
skirts ... pants
Fords ... Chevies
nukes ... anti-nukes

At this level, friendships aren't too deep. Sheer numbers dictate casual acquaintances. It is conceivable that you know a thousand people by name who fit into these categories. You may not hesitate to call them friends. However, knowledge of them is restricted to a short bio, and mutual concern over the distinction that draws you together. It is doubtful you would call any in this group to inform them that your cat died, that you need a loan, or that you will be featured in tonight's 6:00 news.

SECOND—THOSE WHO WOULD ATTEND YOUR
SURPRISE BIRTHDAY PARTY.

This thins the crowd down to a special dozen or two. It is your bowling team, your frat house, the computer club, the exercise gang, or the inner group left over from high school days. Together, they compose the people you spend most of your time with.

You do more than talk politics and weather with these people. You share dreams, explore adventures, conquer trials and laugh through embarrassment together. They build an environment around you that releases you from daily pressures. You use your first name when you call them on the phone. You risk new things, new ideas with them.

23

The main emphasis in this relationship is fun. When life gets too serious, there's always someone in the gang to liven it up for you. They'll campaign for you, and celebrate with you, win or lose.

You can't share everything with this crowd, but that doesn't matter. They make the going easier for you.

THIRD—THOSE YOU WOULD CALL FIRST
WHEN DAD DIES.

When you win those two free tickets to Hawaii, these are the ones from whom you would choose a traveling mate. When you're depressed, they are the only ones you would want to talk to. They are first in line to help you move into that new apartment, or pull you out of a ditch at 3 A.M..

Their mothers call you to find out where they are. They care enough to tell you about the spinach on your teeth. They will push you to the finish line, when you're ready to quit. They alone know how much you resent following in your sibling's footsteps, the real truth about your sex life, why you refuse to ride in airplanes, and your feelings about death.

Most everyone you consider friends fit into one of these three categories. You begin with those on your side of the line. From there, you sort out your gang. Then, you pick two or three closer companions.

The problem comes when we expect high levels of friendship from the wrong people. Just because the multitude is on your side, doesn't mean they will cry when you do.

Failure at friendship can devastate you or harden you, unless you recognize these various levels and make realistic assessments.

For example, take the perfect person. Not many of

those around. The one who would probably be voted into that category by the most people would be Jesus Christ. You remember, the man who did everything right. So, the whole world loved Him?

He drew a well-defined line and a multitude crossed over to His side. However, He did not treat all of them alike. He selected a special group of twelve men. He hand-picked them, and worked at building trust and unity. He only had one dropout. This constituted His special-interest gang.

But even the perfect man enjoyed a few friends who were closer than the twelve. Out of that group He selected James, John, and Peter to experience intimate times, times when He allowed His inner nature and character to show.

Levels of friendship ... we all need them.

SO, WHO CAN YOU COUNT ON?

Good friends have your best interests in mind. They're your fan club, public relations staff, valets, personal psychologists, security blankets, and wardens all rolled into one.

Good friends accept you as you are. This doesn't mean they like everything you do. It does mean they won't desert you, even though you never change. You can cut the phony talk, dress and image. They've seen the warts and said, "It's okay."

Good friends are willing to build a friendship. They take little for granted. They initiate plans for the two of you. They find generosity comes easily. They keep surprising you with their loyalty.

Good friends don't close out the rest of the world for you. You can concentrate on the really close friends, but still enjoy those who are at different levels.

Good friends help you to like yourself. They emphasize your good points, while making you accountable for the bad.

Good friends sometimes drive you crazy. "You know me better than to think that." "I told you not to tell anybody!" "Of course I called the police, I was worried sick about you." "What do you mean, you had a slight accident with my new car?" The closer the friend, the more serious the danger of violation of trust. But the crisis should be short-lived, and could be used to face up to a rough spot in the relationship.

No effort on behalf of this friendship is ever wasted. Every conscious effort to be kind, gentle, helpful and considerate makes you a more kind, gentle, helpful and considerate person. How can you lose?

SORTING THEM OUT

If it is true that you'll have only two or three truly close friends at a time, wouldn't you rather pick out your friends than just fall into relationships? If you like those closest to you to be loyal, creative and adventurous, why become close to someone who is irresponsible, boring and lazy? Take a minute to speculate. List those qualities you believe to be important to you in a friend. It might help to consider one of your existing close friends, and use the following headings to jot down what you admire about them.

INDISPENSIBLE QUALITIES   OPTIONS

Under options, consider: If they are brunette or blonde, would it make a difference? If they were shorter? Taller? If they were a different race? (Think about that one.) If they got better grades? Worse grades? You get the picture.

TEN THINGS YOU CAN DO
TO STRENGTHEN FRIENDSHIPS

For those on your side:

1. Volunteer to head voter registration drives for the political party of your choice.
2. Organize the annual float committee.

For those in the gang:

3. Stage a "come-as-you-wish-you-were" party.
4. Convince the whole bunch to attend a C.P.R. class together.
5. Volunteer your group of "crazies" to come, in costume, to the children's ward of a nearby hospital.

For those special ones:

6. Try out an exchange—visit their work, school, home, etc., for a whole day. Then it's their turn to bird-dog you.
7. Find a skill they have and you don't. Have them teach it to you.
8. Declare a national "Promote My Friend Week," and then go for it. Paint giant fluorescent posters that proclaim, "Tammi Is Terrific!" Write a note to her employer about what a good job she does. Introduce new people to her by saying, "Come meet my good friend, Tammi. I know you're going to like her."
9. Ask your friends to tell you what they think is your weakest character trait or worst habit. Then surprise them by working to change it.
10. Choose one friend, and take a trip, just the two of you. Share some sights, relax a lot, be yourself, dream out loud.

27

How well are you going to be remembered at your class reunion? A lot will depend on how well you build and maintain friendships at all levels.

CHAPTER 3
WILL THEY EVER STOP CALLING ME JUNIOR?

"I'm 22 years old!" John moaned. "What do you mean, 'when I grow up'?"

It was another of the old son-what-are-you-ever-going-to-make-of-yourself lectures. You know the type. They usually ramble like this:

Dad: "How are the computer classes coming?"

Grad: "I'm not taking the computer classes. I'm taking art instead."

Dad: "WHAT!?"

Grad: "I've always wanted to try oils, so when I got a chance to get into the advanced program, I jumped at it ... "

Dad: "Do you mean to tell me we're shelling out $8,000 a year so you can paint daisies?"

Grad: "It's only for one semester ... "

Dad: "Then you're going back to computers?"

Grad: "Well, I've been meaning to tell you ... you see, some of us have gotten together ... well, we think it's now or never ... we'd like to take off for Europe for awhile."

Dad: "MILDRED! Come in here and talk some sense to your kid!"

Caroline's parents thought her new job was great.

She needed money to fix up her old car, plus a new wardrobe as she began college. Waitress at the Pancake Palace didn't rate the top of the line, but it was respectable, and the tips were good.

From time to time, Caroline's dad stopped by for coffee. He was so proud that she got along with everyone so well. That is, until she dragged Mark home. He rode a motorcycle, could use a shave, and had a silver front tooth.

"What kind of guy would pick up a waitress?" he lectured.

"But, Dad, it's me!" Caroline protested. "Besides, he's a really nice guy when you get to know him." To her dad, she picked the wrong one ... again.

Tom found a beautiful 100-watt quadraphonic stereo system, brand new, still in the box, for an incredible $1,600. The speakers alone were worth that much. A lifetime investment.

"Dad, you know that $2,000 inheritance from Grandpa? Since the scholarship's covering my tuition, I thought I'd take advantage of that deal at Stereo Circus."

"A $2,000 stereo?"

"Well, I'd like a solid oak cabinet to set it off ... "

"Forget it. Grandpa wanted that money used for something really important, like a refrigerator or stove, after you're married."

"But, I don't even have a girl friend ... "

"Don't blame me for that. Sheila Simpson has been waiting for years ... "

"Drop it, Dad."

"But, she'd be perfect for you! If you wait too long, she's liable to be taken ... "

"Dad!"

Most everybody has got one ... a family, that is. They may live across the hall, across the street, or across the country. Quality family life, like a quality friendship, takes effort. For the most part, parents attempt this task. Sometimes, you're on your own. Family life remains the touchstone of security and sanity in an otherwise lunatic society.

Quality family living includes:

PRIVACY

Time alone—absolutely solitaire. No interruptions. Apart from siblings, roommates, house guests, parents.

Privacy provides an objective view of who you are. You can't snow yourself. When it is just you and the mirror, there you are, warts and all.

You need privacy when making the big decisions, away from the distractions of confusion, pressure and interference. It is a season to evaluate the contributions other people make to your life.

WHAT SHOULD YOU DO WITH YOUR PRIVACY?

a. Rest—no pressures, no crisis to solve, no conversation, no expectations from others, just a big sigh and time to listen to the inside of your mind.
b. Hide—from friends, relatives, television, books, bills and whatever else chases you through your daily routine.
c. Contemplate—about how things are really going. Are your plans working out? Do you like what you see in yourself, your environment, your rate of progress?
d. Cry—you know what I mean. Get down to in-the-gut sobbing that is not meant to be seen by another soul on earth. If you've never felt that

way, you've got trouble. Everyone needs to care enough about something, or someone, to shed tears.

e. Dream—ask, "What if ... ?" "What if I tried for the Olympics?" "What if I got married?" "What if I bought a Trans-Am?" "What if I flunked physics?" A time to speculate.

f. Plan—to make your dreams come true. What needs to be done first? Second? Draw up a proposed agenda. What does it take to get there?

g. Decide—take a step. Make up your mind, and go for it—or put it on the shelf and forget it.

h. Get lonely—privacy is not a lifestyle, it is an exercise. Stay long enough to look forward to people again.

HOW CAN YOU MAKE PRIVACY WORK FOR YOU?

See to it that everyone you live with has a place of their own—a room, a desk, a corner, a chair, some piece of turf. It could be a place to walk, a mountain to climb, a beach to stroll, a desert cabin.

Plan isolation. Write it into your schedule; it is a necessity you can't do without. Put it on your "things to do" list. Then, close out the world. Shut the door. Unplug the phone. Don't answer the doorbell. Climb until you hear only the breeze. Jog until it is just you and the seagulls.

It is unaccountable time. You don't have to explain to anyone what you're doing, or where you've been. Now, allow others within your household the same privilege.

Record your visions and struggles. Scratch out a diary, journal, or just a notebook. Keep it honest, personal, specific. Keep it private.

Quality family life also includes:

INTIMACY

If privacy is what you do alone, intimacy is what you do with others. The following is an intimacy test for your household. Respond yes or no:

_____ We spend at least thirty minutes a day talking together.

_____ We each spend time at some of the activities of the other members.

_____ It is a major offense to express verbal put-downs.

_____ Within reasonable bounds, there is free access to other members' personal possessions.

_____ Within the last month we participated in an activity which involved each member.

_____ Within the last month we each worked alongside one other member in order to accomplish an important task.

_____ A private survey would reveal a close mutual agreement on what is right and wrong.

_____ No one member dominates our conversation.

_____ We feel free to ask each others' advice on personal matters.

_____ We enjoy making each other look good.

Six or less positive answers point to major faults in family intimacy. If this is your situation, what can you do?

First, turn off the T.V. Television can destroy intimacy, unless you take certain safeguards. Converse often when the T.V. is on. Pledge never to watch it alone, unless you're the only one home.

Second, show up for all meals. Arrive at the table together, and leave together. Put aside the newspaper and your botany notes, and turn down the stereo. Concentrate on each other and the food.

Third, create comfort. Let there be one room where each member of your household can relax together. Save up and buy a recliner, or some beanbag chairs, whatever is takes to ensure everyone a place where they can kick back.

Fourth, initiate "day share." When someone asks you, "How did things go today?" Really tell them. Begin with breakfast, include the ride to school or work, the conversations you had, etc. Give a video-camera view of your day. Now, you don't have to do that every day. But, a once-in-awhile report nourishes intimacy. You can do this by phone or letter when living away from home.

Fifth, volunteer to be part of the support teams. Help the other members of your household to succeed. Be ready to do whatever is within your ability. Eight out of ten families in America need to work on building intimacy. The other two may just be fooling themselves.

MATURITY

Relationships within a family change. As you grow older you relate to other family members in a different way. The transition process in recognizing your peer level with adult parents can be awkward, for both of you. Together, you must grow toward this maturity. Here are some things to deal with:

GUILT MANIPULATION

As a child, it went like this. "Mother, if I don't get a new dress I'll be the shabbiest girl in school. Even Sylvia, who lives on the north side of town, looks nicer than I do."

Which means, "Mom, you should feel depressed and guilty for forcing me to survive in clothes that bring us all public ridicule."

Now that you're older, the argument goes:

"You know how sick Grandma's been feeling. Why don't I fly up and spend the weekend with her? All that snow makes her melancholy."

Which means, "Why don't you finance my skiing weekend? Maybe I'll stop by and see Grandma if I have the time. Anyway, you should be taking better care of her and this is one way to soothe the conscience."

ME-CENTERDNESS

If you're still living at your parents', you have probably noticed that the household cycle does not revolve around you as often as it used to. Mom and Dad have new interests, a newly discovered intimacy of their own. Siblings grow their own way too. There must be give-and-take while you're stretching toward further levels of independence and maturity.

WISDOM DEPENDENCY

To ignore a parent's available counsel can be foolish. But, to plague them with continual questions is a waste of time. "Should I buy a new pair of shoes?" It's up to you. "Would it be best to get the English class completed before I start the night shift?" Only you can decide. "Do you think she'll like this engagement ring?" You're asking your mother? "If I stay out until 3 A.M., do you think I'll make it to work by 7?" Try it, and see.

UNPREDICTABLE BEHAVIOR

Kids start out to go to Kevin's house, and wind

up at Matthew's. They cry to have an ice cream, then toss it aside to go play. They run to the library for "just a minute," and come home after dark.

Maturity involves keeping promises, time commitments, and schedules that involve others. Most businesses have a system of accountability. You punch a clock, check with a receptionist, or perhaps keep a written record yourself. The business operates according to your responsibility.

Volunteer accountability in a family makes for harmony.

SPIRITUALITY

Better Homes and Gardens, a popular family magazine, takes a periodic survey of the American family. While they admit to certain built-in limitations, they do get a broad response.

One question they consistently ask: "What is the greatest threat to family life today?" In 1972 their readers replied "Materialism." In 1977 they answered: "Inattentive parents." The last survey (July 1983) revealed another answer. More of the respondents claim that the absence of religious/spiritual foundations is the greatest threat to families.

This is not an isolated assessment. Noted sociologist George Gilder stated in an article entitled, "Family, Faith, and Economic Progress," published in the April 15, 1983, edition of *National Review*: "The crucial dimension of escaping our current predicament is faith in God and faith in the future."

The spiritual side of man can be ignored, but there is a penalty. Chances are your family has some sort of spiritual foundation. It may be hidden, dormant, or several generations removed.

If discussion of religious values isn't a part of your family life now, how far back do you have to go to discover it? Perhaps a church-going Grandma? A great uncle who was a preacher? A Dad who had a spiritual experience during the war? Many of the principles observed in your home might be based on biblical concepts. Morality, justice, integrity and generosity (to name a few) evolve from dominant religious themes.

The heavy dependency of our founding fathers upon their religious beliefs still guarantees that we may grow up in an environment permeated by spiritual wisdom.

Alex Haley made searching for our "roots" a national pastime. You might like to join in the hunt, and seek your family's religious heritage. The survey that follows can be adapted for you to send to your relatives. Perhaps you have living kin who can push the generations back and answer such questions as these about family members who are no longer alive.

Dear _____,

(Mom, Dad, Grandma, Grandpa, Aunt, Uncle, Second Cousin [twice removed], Shirt-tail Relative, etc.)

I'm conducting a sociological survey of the impact that religion has had in our family. I would appreciate your answers to the following:

1. Did you receive any religious training in your growing years? If so, from whom?

2. In your opinion, how important is religion to the security and well-being of family life in general? Why?

3. Were you ever involved in a leadership role in a

religious setting? When? For how long? What did it entail?

4. At the present time, how important to you is faith? Why?

5. Who was the most religious person you ever met? What stands out in your mind about them?

Enclosed you will find a self-addressed and stamped envelope for your reply. Thanks for your help in this project.

Sincerely,

Your obedient (Wayward, long-lost) son/daughter/nephew/et al.

P.S.—Please send cookies, money, tickets to the Super Bowl, Aunt Louise's address, all of the above.

Quality family life includes an appreciation and understanding of shared spiritual values.

SIBLINGS

Your relationship with your brothers and sisters may be good, not so good, or both, depending on your present situation. Whatever it is, these people can be a great advantage to you. There are three important lessons that can be learned through them.

HOW YOU ARE AT YOUR WORST

It goes like this:

Katie-Marie, your high school senior sister, asks your folks if she can go camping at the beach with some friends. Your parents learn the outing will be co-ed, and unchaperoned. Dad says, "No!"

Lovely Katie-Marie lets out a typical tirade of vindictive verbal ingratitude. She slams her bedroom door and refuses to come to dinner. Then comes the bolt of lightning. You hear Dad tell Mom, "Sometimes Katie-Marie acts just like _____" You, at your worst.

A more direct way you can learn from dear brother or sister, deals with their uncanny ability for the unvarnished truth. Just ask one of them about your hairstyle, clothes, how you handled a certain situation. Brutal honesty every time.

HOW YOUR PARENTS EXPECT YOU TO ACT

If you have older siblings, you've got the best deal. Suppose big brother David forgets to bring home his report card. Finally, after parental prodding, he claims he lost it. They get a duplicate from the school office and discover an *F* in English and a *D* in Spanish. When confronted he replies, "Ah, no big deal."

But the two-hour discourse in the living room that night implants a message in your mind: no *D*'s or *F*'s for you.

HOW YOUR COMMUNITY IMAGE MEASURES UP

"Hey, are you Wally's brother?" the man behind the counter asks.

You timidly/proudly acknowledge the fact, and receive verbal or nonverbal feedback on your status in this man's eyes.

PARENTS

Quality family life means acquiring valuable information from your siblings, but also collecting sage tidbits of life experience from your parents. Just how much do the folks really know? The following can be a guideline.

What brings them to tears? What matters to them enough to move them emotionally?

How much affection do they show for one another? Any couple married twenty-plus years, and still crazy about each other, has a grip on the good life. Listen to them.

How well have they survived crisis? What is their attitude toward "the hard times?"

How readily do they admit mistakes? Have they ever looked you in the eye and said, "Hey, kid, I blew it ... I'm really sorry."

Do they keep promises? If their word is as solid as Fort Knox, then their wisdom is as good as gold.

Are they willing to risk failure? Are they a bit adventurous (but not reckless)? Enjoy new challenges? Would you be shocked if Mom joined the jazzercise class? Or Dad won the office video-game contest? Or decided on a mid-career job change?"

What do the neighbors think about them? Do they ask them for advice or help? Is your home a center of activity?

Perhaps some of these areas are weak, but take full advantage of their example in the strong areas.

You might try some of the following suggestions as a means to strengthen your family life.

Ask the oldest member of the family to tell you in detail about the good old days, and really listen.

Take a problem that you normally see as something you have a right to decide for yourself, and ask the folks, "What would you do if you were in my position?"

List five positive qualities in each of your brothers and sisters. If you're brave, pick out one and ask them how you might improve in that area.

Volunteer to house sit, babysit, dogsit for a whole weekend so that Mom/Dad/brother/sister can have a short vacation.

Say something positive about your parents in a group situation where they can overhear your true feelings.

Tell your folks three things about your home life with them that you hope to re-create in your own home some day.

Family living, in whatever form it takes for you, is an inevitable fact of life. Good family living is crucial as a secure foundation for quality in a complicated age.

Chapter 4
I'd Like To Stop Asking, "How Much Does It Cost?"

What is the best way to make a million bucks before you are thirty? Choose one:

a. Inherit it from Uncle Buford.
b. Win a magazine sweepstakes.
c. Smuggle dope.
d. Invent an inexpensive, failproof computer lock that allows only one user access to the system.
e. Hit fifty home runs per season, and have an earned run average of less than one for eight consecutive years in high school and college.
f. Major in television communications and broadcasting and win the Miss America contest.

If making a million (or more) is your life's goal, then go for it. It can be done. Personally, I have a hard time psyching myself up for such an attempt. For me, it would take more concentration and discipline than an Olympic hopeful, not to mention incredible timing and luck.

There may be more reasonable, and enjoyable, financial ambitions. Here are some possibilities to kick around:

1. I want my finances so soundly established that

43

I can be considered a good credit risk.

2. I want to be financially independent enough that I don't have to sweat each paycheck to keep groceries on the table.

3. I want to be able to purchase at least one of my material dreams (Corvette, cabin near the Tetons, fur coat, South Seas cruise, etc.)

4. I want to have enough cash on hand to be able, on occasion, to assist my friends in emergencies.

5. I want to be able to afford a quality vacation each year (more on that in Chapter 6).

Add your own goals to this list. Each of us will have a diversity of top limits and bottom lines.

Eddie is a senior business major at California State University. He lives at home, works three days a week at a savings and loan, and has been the chief projectionist at the neighborhood theater for over six years. He drives a late-model car, dresses well, likes to eat out, pays all his own expenses, and has just returned from a vacation to the Virgin Islands.

Last month Eddie loaned his friend, Dan, $200 to get his car fixed. Eddie is not wealthy, nor greedy, neither is he a penny-pincher. He is just financially sound, solvent and stable.

Sound money management comes about through a well-developed game plan, sometimes called a budget. While there exist a few rare characters who can keep track of incomes, expenses, and projects in their heads, most of us need it down in writing. The following form could help.

BUDGETING

NET INCOME
Source: Annual   Monthly

_____ $ _____ $ _____

_____   _____   _____

_____   _____   _____

(Include wages, parental supplements, scholarships, gifts)

	Total Annual	Total Monthly
	$ _____	$ _____

EXPENSES	Annual	Monthly
Housing: Rent (dorm costs, house payment, amount paid to parents, etc.)	_____	_____
Utilities	_____	_____
Water, sewer, garbage	_____	_____
Telephone (estimate long distance charges too)	_____	_____
Cable T.V.	_____	_____
Furnishings (now paying on or will need to buy)	_____	_____
Other household expenses	_____	_____
PERSONAL MAINTENANCE		
Food	_____	_____
Clothing Purchases	_____	_____
Repair, cleaning, laundry	_____	_____
Medical (insurance and/or projected doctor, dentist, etc.)	_____	_____
Vanity expenses (hair, cosmetics, etc.)	_____	_____
TRANSPORTATION		
Car payment	_____	_____
Fuel, repairs, maintenance	_____	_____
License, registration, parking, tolls	_____	_____
Bus, plane, cab	_____	_____

Auto insurance   _____   _____

SELF IMPROVEMENT

School
  Tuition   _____   _____

  Fees, books, misc.   _____   _____

Physical care (gym, aerobics class,
  running shoes, backpack, etc.)   _____   _____

Skills advancement (piano lessons,
  exams, etc.)   _____   _____

FUN

Sports, recreation   _____   _____

Restaurants   _____   _____

Hobbies   _____   _____

Movies, shows, concerts   _____   _____

Other   _____   _____

DEBT PAYMENT

School loans   _____   _____

Personal commitments (family, other)   _____   _____

Credit cards, charge accounts   _____   _____

OBLIGATIONS

Dues, charity, church contributions   _____   _____

SAVINGS

Christmas, birthdays, gifts   _____   _____

For major purchase of _____   _____   _____

Emergency fund   _____   _____

Vacations (brief, and extended)   _____   _____

You cannot get ahead until you first know where you are. Take the time to record what you take in and what needs to go out.

One way to achieve your financial goals without raising your income involves knowing the right time of year to make purchases. In Sylvia Porter's

New Money Book for the 80's (Doubleday & Co., Inc., Garden City, New Jersey, 1979, pp. 49-51), she lists the best time of the year to make purchases. Here are a few of her suggestions, with some of my own adaptations:

IF YOU WANT TO BUY	GOOD MONTHS TO TRY
Art supplies	January, February
Bathing suits	After July 4
Bicycles	September, October, January, February
Books	
Popular	January
School	At semester's end
Camping equipment	August
Cars (new)	August, September
(used)	February, November, December
Christmas gifts	Anytime but Christmas
Furniture	January, February, June, August, September
Men's clothing	August, January
School supplies	August, October
Ski equipment	March
Sports equipment	Closing weeks of the season
Stereo	January, February, July
Tires	May, end of August

You can develop your own list. Every time you say, "I wish I had waited until now to buy," jot that information down. Make a personal inventory of the sales patterns for products you use. Even with the patience to wait for the right timing, how do you know if you should buy the merchandise?

R.J. eyed an oversize, graphite tennis racket for almost two years. When he found one on sale for $75 less than the normal price, he was tempted. Yet, he owns three other quality rackets. He is caught in a moment of indecision, facing the buy of a lifetime.

If you find yourself in a similar squeeze, take time to ask some questions of yourself.

		TRUE	FALSE
1.	On a scale of 1 (don't need) to 10 (really, really need), it is obvious this item is a must.	___	___
2.	After careful research I believe this price is good.	___	___
3.	I find it easy to explain the rationale for this purchase to those who know me best.	___	___
4.	This is a current model, so I know it won't be outdated soon.	___	___
5.	This is the best time of year to make this purchase.	___	___
6.	I can tell you exactly what this item costs in at least two other stores.	___	___
7.	I'm convinced that no less-expensive substitute exists, or if it does, its inferiority eliminates considering it.	___	___
8.	I know of other satisfied owners, and/or had a first-hand demonstration.	___	___
9.	The company that makes this product is considered one of the best in the field.	___	___
10.	The retailer from whom I'm purchasing this item has a reputation for integrity.	___	___
11.	The retailer offers special services which enhance the value of this product.	___	___
12.	This costs a chunk, but it will truly satisfy the inner need.	___	___

Use the following grading system:

10-12 True—go get it.
7-9 True—Postpone purchase until more thought.
Under 7 True—No way, adios, forget it!

Take a look at how R.J. applied this system to his racket purchase consideration.

1. False, since he has three other oversize rackets.
2. True, he has checked every ad in the sporting goods section for the past two years.
3. True, his logic: "It is the best, and I've always wanted one." His friends are easily swayed.
4. True, the Prince Graphite is a standard in tour-

nament play and should remain so for years to come.

5. True, found it in October.
6. True, R.J. knows the cost in at least ten other stores.
7. True, R.J. has the inferior models.
8. True, R.J. played three sets last spring with a borrowed Graphite.
9. True, in tennis, the Prince name needs no explanation.
10. True, Santa Clara Pro-Shop has been at Central and Evergreen for thirty-two years.
11. True, free stringing offered that is guaranteed for thirty days.
12. True, owning the best in the field.

R.J. totaled up 11 trues (with #3 and #12 questionable), so he purchased the racket. It hasn't improved his game all that much, but it makes him feel good about himself every time he unzips the cover and wraps his hand around the leather grip.

CAR, CLOTHES, AND FOOD

Three main concerns in the area of economy have to do with car, clothes, and food. A wise money user can gain a jump or two on quality without going broke.

You can afford a quality meal. Here is how. First, estimate the amount you spend monthly for food. For example, say you live alone and spend $120 a month. This means nothing fancy. Just hamburgers, spaghetti, casseroles, etc. Without increasing your budget you could serve a bountiful steak dinner for two.

Cut out the snack foods. (Nutrition will be handled in Chapter 7, right now this is just an economy move.) One less candy bar, Twinkie, or soft drink means 30¢ to 50¢ saved per day. Figured at the lower end, and based on a 5-day snack week (you bum cookies at Mom's on the weekends), you could save $6.00 per month.

Set a limit to eating out—10% of the food budget would be nice. If you live alone, 20% would be acceptable (the average is more like 30%). Say you cut back 10%. That is a decrease of $12.00, and since it is 60% cheaper to eat at home, you should save $7.20 monthly.

When you shop at the grocery store keep these things in mind.

a. Prepare a list, and stick to it. By doing this, you could eliminate a package of carob almonds ($1.43), two containers of French custard yogurt (89¢ each), mustard (62¢) (you already have some), and a $1.36 box of that new cereal you saw advertised on T.V.

b. Never shop when you are hungry. The last time you did, you bought that large box of coconut cookies that got stale before you ate them all (cost, $1.98). You usually reward yourself with a shopping day "treat," even if you aren't hungry, so for the month multiply this times four.

c. Make sure everything in your basket is food or food related. Shop for drugstore items, books and records, etc., at another time. In one month's time, you could easily tack onto your food bill two quarts of oil for the car ($2.32), a paperback novel ($2.50), a record ($7.98), a pair of toenail clippers ($2.15), and two tabloid newspapers (75¢ each).

d. Purchase "no-frills" brands on non-essential items. If the corn is going to be tossed into a tamale pie, why pay 6¢ more per can? If you're making pudding, who cares if it is whole milk, skim milk, or powdered milk? "Buying down" can save you at least $10 per month.

e. Think twice before buying convenience foods.
Even though you want speed in your cooking, pre-
packaged foods clobber your budget. In one month
you could save $1.23 by making homemade waffles,
instead of using frozen. You could save $2.65 by bak-
ing your pizza from scratch, and 23¢ by purchasing
frozen peas without butter.

Closer examination reveals a conservative estimate of the savings—about $56. Almost half the ori-
ginal budget. Sylvia Porter confirms this idea in her
New Money Book for the 80's saying, "The savings I
recorded in a recent experiment of my own amounted
to 41%."

Even if you're a skeptic and take the lower figure
of 41%, then cut it in half and make your savings a
paltry 20% that makes $24. Do you know what that
means? You could prepare a dinner for a special
friend: with the best two steaks on the market, two
huge Idaho baked potatoes, sour cream, chopped
onions (optional), real butter, fresh broccoli, a green
salad with tomatoes, radishes, sprouts and bacon
bits with blue cheese dressing, pick up a $4.00 coco-
nut cream pie at the bakery, and still have enough
money left for aromatic candles. Now, that is quality.
It beats store-bought cupcakes any day.

Now, for your clothes. Again, one enemy is poor
planning. Do you have any idea what you have? Do
an inventory. Make it simple. Divide your wardrobe
into three categories: dress, casual, and grubby. Now,
jot down what you actually need in each category. Include undies, shorts, swimsuits as well.

Keep a list of needed items in your wallet or purse

51

at all times. You never know when you will run into a bargain (that fits, is the right color, season, etc.). Determine not to purchase anything that is not on that list. Resist compulsive buying during rushed morning breaks and shopping on long, rainy afternoons (when there is nothing else to do).

Check the welts on shoes, seams on dresses, and washing instructions on the tag. Never buy "close fits." Don't diet before buying tight pants, or shop for leather shoes early in the morning before your feet naturally widen.

Look for bargains on low-usage items, and quality in high-usage items. For instance, I wear black loafers about six times a year, for not more than an hour or so each time (weddings). I obtain the least expensive pair I can find. They'll be fine. On the other hand, I wear cowboy boots every day of the year. What do I pay? For a pair that fits well, $150.

It helps when you buy off-season, know exactly when you're going to wear the item, and have a tap on the nearest factory outlets, seconds stores, and bargain barns. If you watch your regular purchases, you'll save enough to splurge on a luxury or two for the old wardrobe.

Unless you've already found the perfect car to last a lifetime, this can be an ongoing headache. The virtues of owning a brand new car are obvious. But, for many, the cost is prohibitive. And, we all have our fantasy vehicle. Mine happens to be a full-size, 4-wheel-drive, black pickup with stereo, air conditioning, and standard transmission. Throw in some rugged tires, custom wheels, and dual fuel tanks and I'd be in off-the-road heaven.

I found one of these jewels at a dealership last

week. The price? $15,600.00. The man said it was a true bargain. Only $2,900 more than the red Camaro sitting next to it. I committed myself to looking at used cars.

The latest figures show that standard-size cars depreciate in value by 25% the first year, and another 15% the second. (That doesn't fit all makes and models, but can act as a guide.) This means that the $10,000 limousine you purchase could be worth $6,000 in two years. When figuring your monthly car payment, insurance bill, fuel and upkeep, you must realize your new car's depreciation will cost you an additional $150 per month.

A car two or three years old seems to be an economical target worth your aim. But, how can you be sure you're not getting a lemon? You can't, but you can decrease the odds when you:

KNOW THE LANGUAGE

1. Car size (based on interior cargo and passenger space):

large ... more than 120 feet
mid-size ... 110 to 120 cubic feet
compact ... 100 to 110 cubic feet
subcompact ... 85 to 100 cubic feet
minicompact ... less than 85 cubic feet

2. EPA rating: Fuel consumption under comparable laboratory conditions can be obtained by writing to Fuel Economy, Consumer Information Center, Pueblo, Colorado, 81009.

3. Some newspaper ad abbreviations you should know:

A/C = air conditioning
AT = automatic transmission

cpe = coupe (sporty, two-door)

cyl = cylinders (4, 6, 8, power greater as number increases)

dlr = a car dealer

loaded = has many extras

lo mi = low mileage, subjective

man = manual transmission

pb, ps, pw = power brakes, power steering, power windows

sacr = sacrifice, subjective

sed = sedan, larger than coupe, 2- or 4-door, with closed cargo area

wrnty = still qualifies for factory warranty

PU = pickup

4x = four-wheel drive, rough-terrain, high-mileage vehicle

wgn = station wagon

EXAMINE IT THOROUGHLY

The Reader's Digest *Complete Car Manual* (Wade E. Hoyt, The Reader's Digest Association, Inc., Pleasantville, N.Y. ©1981, p. 17), includes a valuable section on how to buy a used car. A few suggestions:

First, know who you are buying from. If a dealer, check out his reputation; if a private party, check with a mutual acquaintance or neighbor.

Second, give it a visual test. "Never try to buy a used car at night; you need sunlight to spot defects or poor repairs."

Look at the bodywork for signs of dents, rust, worn paint. Check out all the features to see if they work (windows, keys, glove compartment, etc.). Inspect tires for even wear. Take the spare out and inspect it with the others. Don't kick them, but do pull on the tops of front tires to check for excessive movement. Bounce each corner of the car to check shocks. Examine the engine for fluid leaks. Check the trunk area for signs of heavy usage. Look over the interior for wear, investigate funny smells. Press down on the brakes—they should feel firm. Examine the exhaust system for holes, patches, leaks.

Third, give it a road test. Insist on driving the car. Listen for strange noises as you start the engine. Accelerate under different road conditions. Drive on bad roads and around corners. Check the brakes, and every gear in the transmission. When finished, restart the engine while it is hot. Listen again. Look at the engine while it is running to spot leaks.

Fourth, if you think this is the one, hire a mechanic you trust to give it a once-over. It will be worth the investment. There really are many good used cars around. Keep asking questions. If you do not receive satisfactory answers, keep searching.

Cars, clothes, and food. They are immediate expenses. And the day will come to add in house buying, savings accounts, insurance policies, kids, business, boats, and investments. Where do you find trusty principles to guide you in all these money affairs?

Would you believe, the Bible?

That old book has been around for ages, and still contains rich wisdom for your financial deals. Glance through these quotes from the Living Bible:

- Any enterprise is built by wise planning, becomes strong through common sense, and profits wonderfully by keeping abreast of the facts (Proverbs 24:3,4).
- Don't begin until you count the cost (Luke 14:28).
- A prudent man foresees the difficulties ahead and prepares for them; the simpleton goes blindly on

and suffers the consequences (Proverbs 22:3).

- Steady plodding brings prosperity; hasty speculation brings poverty (Proverbs 21:5).
- Riches can disappear fast. And the king's crown
  doesn't stay in his family forever—so watch your
  business interests closely. Know the state of your
  flocks and your herds (Proverbs 27:23,24).
- Pay all your debts (Romans 13:8).
- Just as the rich rule the poor, so the borrower is
  servant to the lender (Proverbs 21:7).
- Unless you have extra cash on hand, don't coun-
  tersign a note. Why risk everything you own?
  They'll even take your bed! (Proverbs 22:26,27).

Quality finances mean not merely accumulating
more wealth, but making sure what you have produces the type of lifestyle you want to pursue.

CHAPTER 5
I'VE GOT TO FIND A JOB
THAT DOESN'T BORE ME TO TEARS

In less than three months it will be all over for Lindy. No more class schedules, teacher's training exams, or term papers. She will be ready to do what she has always planned to do.

At nine years of age, Lindy lined up the neighborhood kids and announced, "Let's play school." She was a born organizer with kind, patient eyes for strugglers, and a stern, no-nonsense expression for the rest. During her freshman year in high school she broadcast with the utmost confidence: "I'm going to be a teacher." Now, close to completing her education, she will begin her dream, her life-long ambition. It is scary.

Oh, she will have no trouble finding a position. She has had three excellent offers. She interviews for another soon. She is not afraid about any of that, or of the future roomful of 10-year-olds. She is sure of her skills—*summa cum laude* sure. And her dedication. But, what is that strange feeling that secretly gnaws at her? It is something she is reluctant to share with most people—maybe, just maybe, she really doesn't want to be a school teacher after all.

How can that be? Here is how she related the story to me.

"I've always been told I'd grow up to be a teacher. And I've assumed so, too. Both Mom and Dad were teachers. The idea was always in the forefront of my thinking. When we had the career guidance course in high school, it was nice that I was one of the few who knew what they wanted to be.

"It just became easier to head in that direction. My folks bragged about what a good teacher I'd make. But all along, I've privately assumed that some Prince Charming would discover me just in time; that I wouldn't really have to teach, and I'd settle down with a family instead.

"The moment of truth has come. There is no Prince Charming, school is almost over, and now my pride won't let me admit that I really have some serious reservations. Good grief, how do you tell your folks that the multi-thousand-dollar education they have given you might be for nothing?"

She watched my reaction, then uncrossed her legs and leaned forward. "It all broke loose inside me last week. There was my mother with her lesson plans— a sight I've grown up with. The lesson plan book old, yellowed, and its pages crammed with notes, clippings, ideas for expansion. And all built on the same basic structure for the past sixteen years. Over, and over, and over. My mind flashes an endless cycle of my own repetitious words, a sea of faces I may not remember, a mountain of dittoed test papers, angry, unsatisfied parents hounding me. Sometimes I feel trapped. No hope of escape."

Lindy isn't the only one. Carrie has changed her major five times. Sam dropped out of school when he found a well-paying job as a welder. Now, several years later, he is unchallenged, restless. Alan has worked six years for an electronics manufacturer. His job is production efficiency. The highlight of his week is Friday night. He lives from weekend to weekend.

No matter how content you are with your career plans, seasonal evaluations assure quality. Consider these key factors.

—*MONEY:* What is the net value of the job? Net value includes the total material benefits: bonus, overtime, stocksharing, discounts, health policies, etc. Subtract expenses like special clothes or uniforms, transportation, meals, and any other unreimbursed expenses connected with the job. Also consider the future. What salary range can I expect in 5 to 10 years? 20 years? Is this quality for me?

—*STATUS:* When you are asked to fill out a credit application, how do you feel about your title? Embarrassed? Proud? Content? Do you find yourself trying to make it sound like something it is not? What would be your future position? Administrative assistant may sound fine at age 23, but what about at age 50? Don't underestimate the power of status. It can affect everything from your physical health to the person you decide to marry.

—*SATISFACTION:* Appraise your target career in the following areas:

a. *Creativity.* Is there room for your skills to mature? Any chance for applying fresh perspectives, ideas? Any opportunity for designing your own program, product or procedure? Look at some who have been in the field a long time. Are they using techniques that you already know?

b. Independence. How much freedom are you allowed? Any flexibility in hours? How tight is supervision?

c. Leadership. Will you be allowed to use your administrative abilities? How much decision-making are you allowed? Are all positions subservient to one authority? Does the job structure include leadership training?

d. Achievement. Would you be able to look back and say, "This is what I've accomplished," or "look how far we've come." Could you say in later years to kids and grandkids, "Did I ever tell you about the time I ... ?

—*EXCITEMENT:* Where is the adventure? It can come from traveling to exotic places, overcoming formidable odds, excelling beyond your contemporaries, meeting new people, exploring unexpected possibilities, etc. You can measure the excitement level by judging how much you anticipate going to work, how many job-related events you look forward to (i.e. the Miami convention, product shows at the Forum, the spring sales promotion, cutting the radio spots, etc.)

—*RELATIONSHIPS:* Most misery, and most happiness, is caused by people, not things. You will need to be around a particular type of people, and your needs will be different from others' needs. Does your work surround you with "your kind of people?" Do you consider them equals? Or do their differences offer you challenges in your growth as a person? Is there room for personal interaction? Is there absence of cliques? Can you develop further relationships outside the work environment?

—*SECURITY:* Will you have constant worry about losing your job? Do you see many job openings of this type listed in the ads? How sound is the company? Do you know and understand the procedure for losing this job? What kind of employee rights, unions, or grievance committees are available? Have others made a lifetime commitment to this kind of work? What is the average length of stay for employees?

—*LIFESCOPE:* Does this career play an integral part in what you see yourself to be? Or, is it an attachment that is tolerated for the sake of income? Is it preparation for something else? Will it blend with future family plans? Or will it conflict with them? Does the location suit you?

Consider each of the seven areas. Perhaps I missed a category that you believe would be important. Add it. In the blanks next to the titles, rate each characteristic in order of priority to you based on a total score of 100 points. For instance, money might count for 60 out of 100 points (then again, is it less? more?).

Robert, a friend of mine, completed his job inventory in this way: Money - 25; Excitement - 20; Lifescope - 15; Satisfaction - 15; Relationships - 10; Status - 10; Security - 5. He has a family to support, so money ranked high. But note: Excitement, lifescope, and satisfaction combined equaled twice the score of money. Robert grabbed a quality job. What does he do? He is a civilian photographer, contracted by the U.S. Navy to shoot high-altitude photos of everything from space shuttle liftoffs, to laser weapon tests, to an occasional reconnaissance layout of foreign military operations.

Another friend, Mike, took the inventory. For him: Lifescope - 30; Satisfaction - 25; Relationships - 25; with Status, Security, Money and Excitement valued at 5 each. His quality job? Living in the mountains of southern Bolivia where he translates the Bible into a native Indian language.

Robert and Mike wouldn't trade their careers for any other. But, to prevent the ruts that anyone can fall into, a continual system of evaluation is essential. Things change. People change. The quality of a vocation can change.

Apply these characteristics to your present job, or to the career you aim for in the future. How do the ideal and the actual compare? If you listed Money as a high 50, and the job you possess provides more like 40, or 30, what can you do about it? If Excitement and Lifescope received 15s, and your job measures up, hang on.

Back to Lindy, my friend with the second thoughts about teaching. Her inventory looked like this:

THE IDEAL		THE ACTUAL	
10	Money	7	Money
15	Status	12	Status
20	Satisfaction	18	Satisfaction
10	Excitement	5	Excitement
20	Relationships	18	Relationships
5	Security	5	Security
20	Lifescope	18	Lifescope
100	TOTAL	83	TOTAL

The "perfect" job choice would equal 100 points. There are few of those around, and the competition is rough. For example, I've always considered the perfect job to be ex-president of the United States. However, the prerequisites for the position don't attract me in the least.

Any job totaling above 90 on the inventory is the chance of a lifetime. Grab it and don't let go.

Anything above 75 fits you. It is something you could give your life's efforts to. Take the job.

If you find yourself between 50 and 75, you could probably survive the daily grind, at least for a while. If it is the best thing available, take it, and keep your eyes open to alternatives. Don't assume you must be locked in forever.

If your job possibility rates below 50, take it *only* to put food on the table, and because nothing else is available (which are valid motivating factors, by the way). Meanwhile, actively seek the training and/or opportunities to transfer out.

This thought process helped Lindy to realize that, indeed, teaching did promise a good career for her. She needed the assurance that she had the actual desire and had made her own decision. She then rated her three job possibilities with the same inventory and determined which suited her best.

Now, how do you keep and maintain a quality job, as well as find one? This requires a fine-tuning of skills in the following areas:

KNOW WHAT IS OUT THERE

Unless you stumbled onto a 90-plus job your first venture out, you will want to keep tabs on the available markets. The situation quickly changes. A *Fortune* magazine article (May 16, 1983) predicted the "Jobs of the 1990s," might be ...

    a. Food services for those who don't eat at home— 6.4 million workers needed, a 32 percent increase in the next ten years.

b. Health care—2.7 million new jobs, the largest projected gain in any field.

c. Economists—42 percent more than are now at work.

d. Secretaries—nearly a million more will be needed in the next ten years. Familiarity with word processors, computers and complex information systems may be required.

e. Waste management—quality control chemists and environmental engineers.

f. Lasers—an expanding industry that could truly explode (no pun intended) on the job market. Electrical engineers with laser backgrounds will find open fields.

g. Real estate—the baby boomers have grown up and want to buy houses, 34 percent more jobs in this field.

h. Fiber optics—the telecommunications field is busily converting to optical cables drawn by glass rods. Physicists and engineers will continue to be needed in great supply.

There are two drawbacks to trying to outguess the potential job market. First, you'll always be one step behind. I just referred to the May '83 *Fortune* magazine. What month and year is it now, as you read this book? My information may very well be outdated.

Any book works that way. Words typed by an author appear in print more than a year later. Magazines speed the process somewhat. Most feature stories are written four to six months before they appear on the rack. Current trends can be found in daily papers such as *The Wall Street Journal*.

The second drawback is that you may not care about the newest innovations in career choices. Your idea of quality could be handcrafting leather belts or manufacturing wood stoves.

Peter studies to be proficient in underwater medicine. He hopes to bring emergency care to divers who construct off-shore oil well rigs. There will be no stampede to join him, nor will he find such an opportunity listed in a magazine. Yet, for him, it is a quality vocation.

KNOW HOW TO GET IT

It doesn't matter whether you are pounding the pavement for your first interview, or you have changed occupations six times already; you have to know what it takes to land the job.

a. Research: If you'll be approaching a major corporation, spend an afternoon in a library to bone up on pertinent information. Check the *Reader's Guide to Periodical Literature.*

If it is a local concern, ask some knowledgeable friends about the employer. Check with the local Chamber of Commerce and the Better Business Bureau. Study the Yellow Pages to see who the competition is. Find out how long the company has been in business and what kind of long-range plans they have. Ask for the annual reports for the last several years. Read the job description ahead of time. If none is offered, ask them to make up one.

Ask plenty of questions. Make a list and keep it handy. Investigate the salary and benefits. Hunt for hidden responsibilities and expenses. If possible, talk with the person who previously held the position. Find out who you will be working under, and what they are like. Get as complete a view as possible and the full scope of the job.

b. Impact: What should be the first impression you give to those hiring? Find out if it is important whether you show up in jeans or a suit and tie. You should look and act like the type of person they normally hire. If that is offensive to you, then don't bother with the interview. Be positive, upbeat. You want to convince them you're just the kind of person they could work with for years to come.

If your first impact will come through a written dossier, take a lesson from my friend, the computer programmer. He is on his way up. He always seems to get the position he wants. One secret is the design of his resume.

His dossier is compact, yet informative. It is written in an easy-to-scan manner. Every date, name, and phone number is correct. Every reference is current. When complete, he takes it to a printer. Not an "instant" place, but a regular typeset printing company. He picks out quality paper, buys matching envelopes, and uses boldface sectional headlines with justified right margins. The whole project costs him $100 for 50 copies. He upgrades it every few years, whether he is looking for a job change or not. That way he is ready when that 90-plus job opening jumps out at him.

Think of it from the employer's point of view. He is sitting there with 75 resumes on his desk. He wants to eliminate all but six or seven. The stack includes some that are handwritten, some just brief paragraphs, others 10 pages long, a few frayed around the edges, several with glaring grammatical or typing errors, and some with names crossed off and new ones added.

Then, suddenly there in the middle, sparkles a jewel. It is printed professionally, easy to read, on beautiful 25% cotton bond paper. (If he holds it up to the light, he can detect the watermark.) That doesn't guarantee a job, but it certainly increases the chance of a personal interview. It is called impact.

c. *Substance:* Sell yourself, but not with a snow job, or high-pressure pitches. For one thing, it would be too tiring to try to live up to that kind of image after you got the job. For another, most times they'll see right through it.

Let them know solid, reasonable, confirmable facts about why you are the right one for the job. Get to the point, ask your questions, make sure they understand with what care you're considering this option. Be businesslike, be human—allowing a full glimpse of your personality. Be sincere and willing to develop rapport with the interviewer, whether you get the job or not.

Margie was turned down for a job as a copy editor at a Chicago publishing house. Two months later, she got a call from the editor-in-chief, who offered her a place in the public relations department. He remembered her long after the interview.

KNOW HOW TO ADVANCE

Most jobs begin well. But sometimes, even the best of jobs stagnate. You wonder if you are stuck with less than quality. Aiming for a better position could be the answer.

But that might require additional skills or training. Most corporate executives possess a master's degree, in addition to their business or engineering degree. Are you ready for night school? Or correspondence courses? Or using your vacation time inside a classroom?

Another way to advance is to do an exceptional job at your current level. Demonstrate your competence for bigger things, in tough situations. Let the boss know you're interested in something more.

When Sally learned that the manager of her travel agency branch needed to speak fluent Spanish, she enrolled in a Berlitz course. When the position opened, she was the most likely candidate.

KNOW HOW TO QUIT

Kenny Rogers sings it, "You gotta know when to fold 'em ... " Sound easy? It isn't. You know it is time to quit:

1. when you've got another job;
2. when it is most convenient for your present employer;
3. when you can do it with the least amount of enemies;
4. when the present job threatens your physical/mental health;
5. when you're forced to violate personal, moral or ethical standards.

So, how do you quit?

With dignity. Burn no bridges—with the organization or any individual. Quit with reasonableness. Describe why, what steps led you to this point. Speak directly to the supervisor; don't let him hear through the grapevine.

Make it final. Finish as many projects as possible. Make sure others know what you're leaving undone. Give an exact date of departure. Share your plans for the future. Let those who have benefited you know about it and thank them.

KEEP YOUR CAREER
IN PROPER PERSPECTIVE

Some time, perhaps in the heavy stillness of a dark night, you'll wonder to yourself, why do I do this? Even with a quality job, and an exciting, secure future, you'll ask yourself, is this all there is to life? Life is surely more than just work and career advancement. But, what is it?

Douglas Adams, in his hilarious international bestsellers (*The Hitchhiker's Guide to the Galaxy,* New York, Harmony Books, 1979, *The Restaurant at the End of the Universe,* loc. cit., 1980, *Life, The Universe, and Everything,* loc. cit., 1982), continually asks the question, "What is the meaning of life?" His answer is the sum: 42. Absurd. Not the kind of thing to satisfy the deep yearnings of the soul, but it does elicit a laugh or two. Seriously, though, where is your life heading?

It is a question that has been asked for a long time. Listen to this:

> I said to myself, "Come now, be merry; enjoy yourself to the full." But I found that this, too, was futile. For it is silly to be laughing all the time; what good does it do? So, after a lot of thinking, I decided to try the road of drink, while still holding steadily to my course of seeking wisdom. Next I changed my course again and followed the path of folly, so that I could experience the only happiness most men have throughout their lives.
>
> Then I tried to find fulfillment by inaugurating a great public works program: homes, vineyards, gar-

dens, parks and orchards for myself, and reservoirs to hold the water to irrigate my plantations. Next I bought slaves, both men and women, and others were born within my household. I also bred great herds and flocks, more than any of the kings before me. I collected silver and gold as taxes from many kings and provinces.

In the cultural arts, I organized men's and women's choirs and orchestras. And then there were my many beautiful concubines. So I became greater than any of the kings in Jerusalem before me, and with it all I remained clear-eyed, so that I could evaluate all these things. Anything I wanted, I took, and did not restrain myself from any joy. I even found great pleasure in hard word. This pleasure was, indeed, my only reward for all my labors.

But as I looked at everything I had tried, it was all so useless, a chasing of the wind, and there was nothing really worthwhile anywhere. Now I began a study of the comparative virtues of wisdom and folly, and anyone else would come to the same conclusion I did that wisdom is of more value than foolishness, just as light is better than darkness; for the wise man sees, while the fool is blind. And yet I noticed that there was one thing that happened to wise and foolish alike—just as the fool will die, so will I. Then I realized that even wisdom is futile. For the wise and fool both die, and in the days to come both will be long forgotten.

So now I hate life because it is all so irrational; all is foolishness, chasing the wind. And I am disgusted about this, that I must leave the fruits of all my hard work to others. And who can tell whether my son will be a wise man or a fool? And yet all I have will be given to him—how discouraging!

The author? King Solomon of Judea, nearly 3,000

years ago (Ecclesiastes 2:1-19, LB).

Whether it is found in the Bible, or in yesterday's newspaper, the question is still the same: Is this all there is? You'll probably attempt to push aside such an annoying, haunting question. However, it'll pop up when you least expect it, a leviathan you hoped was extinct.

The authors of the Bible discovered answers, too, as well as asking questions. And after all these years, their answers still hold. Jeremiah said,

> Thus says the Lord, "Let not a wise man boast of his wisdom, and let not the mighty man boast of his might, let not a rich man boast of his riches; but let him who boasts boast of this, that he understands and knows Me" (Jeremiah 9:23,24a NASB).

A quality career makes up a large part of a quality life, but it is not everything.

CHAPTER 6
WHY WATCH TELEVISION ALONE?

Nate figured on a light weekend.

It was. A rare event—no homework, no overtime on the job, and too early for term papers or exams. But to ease his conscience, he determined to do a little "search and seizure." This is his phrase for skimming through a book and pulling out the kinds of facts professors delight in sprinkling through test questions.

Friday morning Nate scribbled a note on the fridge, "Let's do something big tonight!" He looked forward to some laughs with his three roommates. Wrong.

Aaron decided to go home to see him mother. Jed left after work to go down to the state fairgrounds, because he wanted an early entry in the rodeo. Danny claimed he needed to study at the library.

"Danny," Nate protested, "you've never studied there before!"

"I'm turning over a new leaf. Decided to get a jump on that anthropology paper. But how about later? Say, nine o'clock? Besides, it's your day to go to the laundromat, remember?"

Terrific. Three hours in a dirty, dingy laundromat. Nate did go, and he bumped into a guy from his Lit.

class. He griped to Nate that he had been called to work that evening and was now stuck with a couple of tickets to the rock concert at the Convention Center. Nate grabbed them. The concert had been sold out for weeks.

Nate juggled the bundles of laundry into the living room and found Danny home early from the library. "This is the most exciting night of my life," Danny shouted as he pulled out one of his shirts from Nate's pile and ran to the shower.

Nate trailed after him. "Hey, Danny, I met this..."

"It's incredible," Danny interrupted. "You're now talking to a guy who landed a date with none other than Suzanne Brownfield."

"*THE* Suzanne Brownfield ... Miss Campus Cutie for September? ... Miss 10+? ... Miss Dolly Clone? ... YOU?," Nate was impressed.

"Didn't I tell you I was going to the library, and turning over a new leaf? It sure paid off."

"When? Where? How?" Nate dropped the bundles on the floor.

"In the library—right next to the Primitive Man section. Anyway, got to hurry ... going to pick her up in an hour. Say, Nate," Danny yelled above the roar of the shower, "you got an extra $10?"

"No, but I got these extra tickets for the rock concert ... do you know someone who might like to go?"

"Tickets? Rock concert? Hey, that would be just perfect for my big debut with Suzanne. How about it, pal?"

"But, I was looking forward to going ... "

"Hey, don't fail me now. If you do, I'll lock up all my magazines, I'll leave my wet towel in the hamper all week, I'll ... "

74

"Come on, Danny, knock it off ... "

"Thanks, Nate. You have made me the happiest man on campus, maybe in the whole state. I'll pay you back the end of the month. Suzanne ... the rock concert ... I think I've died and gone to heaven." He turned off the shower. "Oh, I forgot, I'll need to borrow your car. Aaron took mine. Figured it would be all right."

It wasn't. But the night was shot anyway.

Saturday night proved to be the same. Nate hunched before the T.V. with a two-liter bottle of cola and a box of Yum-Yums. Cheers.

The telephone blasted him awake on Sunday morning. Danny was called to work. Jed made it to the finals for the day's events. Nate thought of a couple of girls he would like to spend the day with, but he didn't dare call them this late. So he succumbed and pulled out his books. So much for his leisure time. Big deal.

Are you having more leisure time and enjoying it less? Sociologists claim this syndrome will prevail more and more in our society. There is nothing quality about watching T.V. alone. But what do you do with that extra time?

CHANGE

Everybody needs a break. If you're always cramming to meet deadlines, you need some open-ended, unhurried time. If you're always intensely involved with people, you need some isolation, away from crowds. If you spend a lot of time alone, you need a party, you need social interaction. If you're addicted to a schedule, you need to leave your watch at home.

REST

The Bible says that God worked six days to create the world, then he rested. If He took time to rest, why shouldn't you and I? Maybe you just need to catch up on your sleep. Or, you need to clear your mind of pressing problems. It can mean catching your breath, assessing where you've gone, or plotting where you're going. It can provide a period of concentration on the big questions: Who am I? What is my purpose in existing? Where is this old world heading? Is there life after death? Is there a God? How do I know what is really true? Who should I believe?

ADVENTURE

Most of your weeks are based on a structure established by someone else, whether an employer or professor or family or friends. You're even controlled by your own habits: the same routes to work or school, the same gas station, the same restaurant or grocery store, the same people, and the same topics. Break away from all that into some fresh unknown.

EXERCISE

If you work every day as a physical fitness instructor, forget this one. All the rest of us need to tone muscles, keep the pounds off, get the heart pumping, and generally re-energize the old bod.

GROWTH

Most people are bored because they are boring, stagnant. You can be the best in your field, but if that is all you know.... Who wants to spend the weekend recapping the arbitrary verb structure of aborigine hunters, or reviewing the 1927 World Series statistics? You need to learn new skills, new facts.

Quality leisure time involves each of the above, but you still have to watch out for a number of enemies that can change quality to boredom at a moment's notice.

Television constitutes quality leisure's number one foe. It doesn't matter what you watch, large doses dull the senses. We sedate little kids and elderly people in convalescent homes with it, why should we think it affects us in a different way?

Lack of planning insures tedium. An old film that gained some honors, "Marty," portrayed two principals who repleated a phrase that has become an American cliché.

"What do you want to do tonight?"

"I don't know, Marty, what do you want to do?"

Don't spend all your time saying, "What do you want to do?" Do something instead! Head in some direction. Make a choice. Mull over your idea of quality leisure, and initiate events to get there.

Of course, there is the vexation of *unreasonable expectations*. If your idea of quality leisure is a two-week cruise on a luxury liner with a ship full of bikinis or hunks, perhaps, just perhaps, you're reaching too high. Quality leisure pops up in all sorts of time frames and places. It can cost $20 or $2,000 or nothing. You can be alone, with someone special, with the gang, or plopped down in a stadium of strangers.

Leisure happens on hillsides, at kitchen tables, even in garages. Just depends on the person. My quality leisure could be your headache.

If you're at a poverty level, be honest. Quality leisure takes more work when you're broke. I know all about the cheap things to do for a weekend. I've read the "Dates Without A Dime" columns, too. I'm not totally convinced. I've had money for leisure, and I've had no money at all. Money is better. Poverty level leisure usually comes, however, on the heels of lack of planning.

Home work (I split the word on purpose) is another opponent of leisure. For some, college is one big party. For others, their job is a continuing entertainment hour. However, those types seldom explore quality living. Then, there are the pre-workaholics. They live and breathe school and work. They can't avoid bringing the class/job home with them. They sacrifice leisure for success as they punch for promotions and grades.

Try an experiment. Take a 2x3-foot piece of posterboard. Label it at the top: "IF I HAD ... " Then make four categories down the side: An Hour, An Evening, A Day, A Weekend.

Here is a sample of my own leisure planner:

IF I HAD ...

An Hour
    lift weights
    shoot three games of pool
    turn off lights, lay on floor with earphones, and
        listen to Barbara Mandrell tape
    flip through magazine at library
    watch an oil painting lesson on P.B.S.

An Evening
    rent video movies (Rocky I, II, and III)
    read a Louis L'Amour novel

play bridge with Jan, Mike and Russ
sketch houseplans for dream house
check out new cars at dealership

A Day
play golf at Palm Springs
go horseback riding at the beach
build a stereo cabinet
take an emergency first-aid class
hike to the top of Pine Mountain

A Weekend
camp in the desert
paint and wallpaper my bedroom
go to Channel Islands National Park
white-water raft down the Kern River

This is your short-term leisure schedule planner. Leave more space under hour than evening, more space under evening than day, and so forth. List as many things as you can think of, both wild and sane. Leave room for later additions. When you read or hear about someone doing something that attracts you, write it down. Once you've done any of the activities, draw a red circle around those you would like to try again, and a black line through things that were a wipeout.

If someone scoops you about a great new Italian restaurant, jot down "Dinner at Alfonso's." If you see a new store opening at the shopping center, list "Check out Sports Thrift." Tape the poster to the inside of your bedroom door, with a pencil close by. Tie it on with a string, if necessary. No excuses for not writing the notions down when they come.

Now, if some leisure time grabs me unexpectedly, I'll know just what to do.

Then, how about the greater chunks of time? Such as a whole week? Or two? Or more? In every case, you'll want to remember planning. In fact, planning a yearly vacation is a good way to spend a leisure day or evening.

GET GOING

Apply for a passport and leave the country. Why wait until you can't see, hear, or taste as well as you can now? Take eight days to visit London, or tour Italy by train, or visit the Salzburg Festival in Austria or the barge canals of France. Divide the cost by the number of paychecks you'll get between now and then, and sock it away.

If you want a real bargain, look no further than south of the border. Mexico offers great values, but gets booked up early. If you can't get what you want at Mazatlan, Puerto Vallarta or Acapulco, try Cabo San Lucas, La Paz, or Ixtapa. I hear reports of a great, yet inexpensive, eight-day Mexico City-Colonial Mexico-Guadalajara trip that includes good hotels, most meals, and such cities as San Miguel de Allende, Guanajuato, and Patzcuaro.

Hawaii and Alaska startle the senses. And don't forget the other 48 states. There is Lake Tahoe on the California/Nevada border; Walt Disney World or EPCOT Center in Florida; or white-water rafting from Jackson, Wyoming; schooner sailing off the coast of Maine; and prairie schooner excursions from North Platte, Nebraska (really!).

Some good ways to cut the costs of your Big Trip are to go off-season, go with a tour group, or go remote.

Off-season travel always makes sense. Deluxe accommodations become available at regular prices. You avoid the crowds. Desert resorts and ski villages have special summer packages. For instance, Sun Valley in Idaho is a terrific spot for summer tennis. Palm Springs, California, empties out during June, July, and August. (Sure, it is over 100° in the shade. Just pop out for a quick swim and tan, then back into the air-conditioned luxury hotel.)

Tour groups save money compared to lone travel, especially if you are crossing the seas. Talk it over with a travel agency. Check out the reputation of the tour operator with several different agencies.

Other things to check out ...

What are the penalties and refunds if you cancel your trip? What are the privileges and options if they cancel the tour? Is the company bonded, or does it have an escrow account? Do you know the hotel rating system? ("First Class" in the U.S. = "Superior Deluxe" on the European continent. Their "First Class" is much lower on the totem.)

Have your read the fine print on the travel brochure? Check for baggage size, costs of side trips, etc., that you assumed were included in total price. What are the door-to-door costs? What meals are provided? How much food is included in the continental breakfast? What tips are included in the statement, "all tips included" (which usually does not mean ALL tips)?

Another cost-cutter and crowd-avoider is the Big Trip to a remote corner of the world. If Yosemite National Park is crammed (and it always is in the summer), try Lassen National Park a few hours north. If skiing at Sun Valley, Idaho, is too expensive, try Mc-

Call, Idaho (where all the natives go).

If a trip to Paris could send you to the poorhouse, try a week in Montreal, or the French Quarter of New Orleans. Unless, of course, prestige and status equal quality for you.

GET PHYSICAL

"Sweat travel" is a booming business. Here are some of the possibilities listed in the *U.S. News & World Report* (May 2, 1983):

1. Bike tours of Vermont and New England include inns, swimming holes, meals, and a "sag" wagon for those who can't keep up. Similar tours reported available in Europe, Israel, New Zealand and Mongolia.
2. There is a jogger-aerobics symposium at Kiawah Island, South Carolina. Many other resorts offer special "runner holidays."
3. Cross-country ski through Norway.
4. Try a kayak trip on Glacier Bay, Alaska.
5. Climb a volcano in Mexico. Popocatepetl and Ixtaxihuatl offer reasonable rates.
6. White-water raft in Papua New Guinea (or Zambia, Chile, Turkey).
7. Hike through the Semien Highlands of Ethiopia or across the Pindos Mountains of Greece.

Even if you don't return rested, at least you'll be in good shape.

GET HOSTEL

A youth hostel, that is, that worldwide network of inexpensive dormitory-style housing facilities. Stay overnight for $5, and it might include a kitchen as well. Grab your camping gear and you're set. All you need is a pass from American Youth Hostels (AYH National Campus, Delaphane, Virginia 22025). A good way to see Europe, Hawaii, or the rest of the U.S.A.

GET LOST

If you haven't discovered the joys of camping, why not give it a try? That is, if excitement, accomplishment and serenity appeal to you. Suggested gear to buy or borrow is:

    a. backpack—lightweight, padded straps, waist belt, waterproof sleeping bag, good quality, nylon, Halofil, or the like (down not necessary at all);

    b. hiking shoes—the new high-top tennies with hiking soles are inexpensive and will get you most places;

    c. assorted gear—stove, canteen, cook kit, first aid, etc.;

    d. friend—who has hiked before and is willing to take you on your first trip.

National Forest Maps are available from your nearest ranger station; topographical maps from the U.S. Geological Survey, Denver, Colorado, 80225, and hundreds of detailed backpack trip books can be obtained at your local sporting goods store.

If you've never scooted across a wooded ridge, hiked to the top of a mountain peak, or listened to the night sounds in a nearly deserted forest, you may not have experienced real quality as yet.

GET BACK TO SCHOOL

What? The last place you would look for a quality

vacation?

Over 180 colleges and universities in the United States and Canada seek vacation travelers. They provide lodging, as well as recreational and cultural facilities. Plenty of entertainment opportunities in the surrounding communities too. Read all about it in *Guide To Low-Cost Vacations And Lodging On College Campuses* at a bookstore, or order from CMG Publications, Box 630, Princeton, New Jersey 08540.

Can a person have too much leisure? Not if it is quality leisure.

Become an *unrelated expert.* Keep searching for that hobby that is totally unrelated to anything you *have* to do at school or on the job. Are you a secretary? Don't type manuscripts. Collect and polish rocks instead. Do you coach basketball? Collect stamps at home. Are you an English major? Take as many geology classes as you can, just for fun.

Develop expertise in an area different from your daily grind in order to become a person you like to be with.

Secure a *leisure partner.* A good leisure partner has the same interests you do, puts leisure time in the same perspective, and has concurrent blocks of leisure time. Qualities I look for in a leisure-time partner include intensity, humor, skill, sense of adventure and reliability.

Develop *monthly madness.* Once a month do one of those things that you've always said, "Hey, you know what would be fun to do sometime?"

A couple of friends of mine rent a video camera every so often and take it out to the Los Angeles airport. One of them dresses like someone important. The other pretends to be a television reporter. They love to watch people's reactions. They relive the hilarity at home with the video tape.

Marlene dressed up in a gorilla suit to meet her roommate at the bus depot. Murph once walked through the drive-through line at a hamburger chain while imitating a sports car (Ruden, ruden, rudeeeeenn ... "chocolate shake, please").

Cherish the *little pleasures*. It is pretty hard not to enjoy a first-class tour of the Caribbean. But don't forget those mini glimpses of leisure: the aroma of a rose; watching big-eyed pre-schoolers as a fire engine screeches by; the hand on your shoulder that says, "Hey, we're on your side"; that haunting melody that lulls you into another world; the gentle Spring breezes. It is pure quality.

Be a *leisure enabler*. Consider others. Help them out in their struggle to get some quality leisure. Help them discover the time, the talent, the means. Share your tips on quality leisure.

Be a *thanks giver*. Don't take quality leisure for granted. Thank your tennis partner for the game. Thank the waitress for the service (include a tip). And thank God for the inspiring sunsets and sunrises.

CHAPTER 7
SURE I CARE ABOUT WHAT I EAT...
BUT NOT VERY MUCH!

The tabloid ad impressed me—a wonder pill that would reduce weight. Scientific reports and numerous case histories presented. There was even a picture of the discoverer included—a kindly old gentleman in a doctor's smock, listed as "one of America's leading nutritionists."

Since I'm not a nutritionist, who was I to challenge an expert? However, the whole thing seemed hard to believe. I decided to do a little checking around. What kind of authority really was making these claims?

In a provocative book entitled *The 100% Natural Purely Organic, Cholesterol-Free, Megavitamin, Low-Carbohydrate Nutrition Hoax* (Whelan and Stare, New York: Atheneum Publishers, Inc., 1983), I discovered the legality of anyone calling himself or herself a "nutritionist": If you completed Nutrition 134 (whether you passed it or not), you're a nutritionist.

There exist legitimate nutritionists too. You'll find them as members of the American Board of Nutrition, the American Insitute of Nutrition, the American Society for Clinical Nutrition, and anyone who is an R.D., registered dietician. However, the ease of becoming an "expert" leads to such a wide variety of opinions, often widely publicized, that finding true facts turns into near impossibility. So, how to evaluate the myriad of claims that assault us from every possible source?

First, evaluate credibility. You certainly know there are degrees, and there are degrees. Some you receive in the mail for $20 ($50 for a doctorate). Some you award yourself. Some come with hard work. "Dr." can mean medical practitioner, an anthropology professor, a psychologist, local mechanic (advertised as the "car doctor), or a popular disc jockey ("Doctor Disgusting").

Find folks with legitimate credentials, or who quote from recognized sources. If you don't know the background, contact the people and ask them for that information. If they don't supply it, consider that part of your answer. You'll find a listing of American Universities and Colleges in your library. It's just as interesting to note what you *don't* find in there.

Second, judge the source's accountability. Who do they answer to? The patent medicine salesmen of another era still abound. They've sophisticated their methods. They no longer stand at the backs of wagons. Now they publicize in newspapers and television. They even write books, and appear on talk shows.

Search for those responsible to a university, or medical society, or, at the least, to public opinion. For instance, an article in a huge national magazine like *Good Housekeeping* should tend to be more accurate than the full-page advertisement in the supermarket rag sheet. Inaccuracies in the article stir hostile letters to the editor, retractions, counter articles, even lawsuits. The ad usually brings big bucks.

Third, sift through the motives. Why should they represent such views? Experts hired by the producer will naturally publish reports designed to boost production. Authors make claims designed to sell books. Store owners slant recommendations to clear shelves, even when they own health food stores, or unhealth food stores. (More on that later.)

But, motives defy detection in many cases. As an example, here is what David Reuben, psychiatrist, physician, and widely published author, explains about the government watchdog, the Food and Drug Administration:

> The leading lights are usually a group of past or future employees of the giant food processors who stop off at the FDA to make friends or learn the ropes. The director of the FDA is usually a political appointee with no technical knowledge of food or drugs. (*Everything You Always Wanted To Know About Nutrition*, Simon & Schuster, 1978, p. 247).

Reuben also says:

> What about the scientific experts at the FDA? The FDA relies heavily on a private group called "The National Academy of Sciences." Actually the NAS is a group of about 100 very capable and distinguished American scientists. But most of them never get within a mile of the FDA offices. The FDA uses a subgroup of the NAS called "The National Research Council." From that small segment they hand-pick a special little group called—more humor—"The Food Protection Committee."

Reuben indulges in some sarcasm:

> That Food Protection Committee is entirely impar-

tial. Just because major food companies contribute up to $100,000 a year toward the "expense" of the committee shouldn't make you suspicious. Just because some of the committee members work full-time for the food manufacturers they are supposed to control—well, that doesn't affect their judgment either. Their bosses wouldn't mind if they made a decision that cost the company a lot of money, would they? Of course not" (paes 248, 249).

Pure motives are as difficult to find as pure food.

Fourth, size up recurring themes. In the flood of advice about what you should eat, and what you shouldn't, what keeps coming to the surface? There is some agreement on values and hazards. I picked up such themes in my own investigations:

a. Beware of white sugar, white flour, white rice.
b. Fresh is best (meat, vegetables, fruit).
c. Most snack foods are out.
d. Only medical doctors (especially those with nutrition backgrounds) can really tell you how much vitamin/mineral supplements you need (if at all).
e. Improper eating makes you feel sluggish, depressed.
f. Soda is a time bomb that can't avoid harming your body (I hate this one).

These are, I repeat, recurring themes only, and should be checked out closely. Off-the-wall statements from a single source don't deserve your attention.

Fifth, use the old common sense. Most promoters of nutrition, on either side of the debate, assume that you and I are unsuspecting simpletons with no ability to discern truth. Like benevolent dictators they propel us into their block of wisdom. The main ingredient I find missing from most of the geniuses is common sense.

One promotion for an "organic" fad diet uses this kind of logic:

In 1880, before the onslaught of modern unhealthy processed food, 250 percent fewer persons per 100,000 died from cancer. In primitive tribes today, where everything is strictly "natural," they have drastically fewer cases of the fatal diseases than we do. And, zoo keepers never feed refined or processed food to their animals because it's so obviously detrimental.

But, I keep wondering ... why is it that the life expectancy in 1880 was about 59? And primitive people seldom reached the age of 40? And zebras die by the time they're 17?

Another bit of common sense ... reading labels on products. What do such terms as "new," "improved," "fortified," "enriched," "natural," "organic," "nature's own," etc., really mean? They seem to me to be nothing more than sales pitches, fitting the same category as Uncle Jethro's Miracle Magic: "Guaranteed to cure consumption, shivers, monthly infirmities, warts and baldness."

We also now know that corn syrup, fructose, dextrose (and all the other ... *ose*'s) are code words for sugar. And, we know better than to believe that every ingredient is listed on the label.

Common sense also warns us that any company that spends more time on the container than on the product cares little about nutrition.

Sixth, enjoy yourself. Try an experiment. Enter into a local health food store, and watch the people.

How happy do they look? I've found a number who appear frantic, desperate, depressed. They're always looking for the right vitamin balance, terrified of hidden additives, neurotic in their quest for purity.

Now, visit an ice cream parlor. The one which features those whopping banana splits and hot fudge sundaes. Watch the expressions of the customers as they plunge their spoons down into the whipped cream and chopped nuts, then scoop up an overflowing river of melted fudge and ice cream. Nothing but smiles and happy sighs. That's fun!

One pundit commented that only fat people die happy. That is not true, of course, but there is a balance. If eating healthy means a long life of paranoid shopping and gaggy ingestions, then it is the short, happy life for me.

Set your own standards, accept the consequences, and enjoy yourself. The old-timers in the Bible had a rational approach:

> So I conclude that, first, there is nothing better for a man than to be happy and to enjoy himself as long as he can; and second, that he should eat and drink and enjoy the fruits of his labors, for these are gifts from God. (Ecclesiastes 3:12, 13, LB)

I don't have a lot of clear answers to the current controversies about the healthiness of modern food, but I do have plenty of questions. As you search for your own balance, consider the validity of these:

IS IT TRUE THAT ...
* Protein deficiency is probably the least common of all major nutrition deficiencies in the United States? Some studies incidate that Americans average 3 to 5 times more protein than needed.

- Fat is a necessary ingredient for a good, healthy diet? It transports vitamins A, C and E; insulates and pads the body and vital organisms; and supplies fatty acids.
- It is nearly impossible in our society for an adult to be deficient in Vitamin E? And overdoses of E produce headaches, low blood sugar, and upset stomachs?
- Some food additives like calcium propionate, are totally natural compounds, and not man-made: Calcium propionate, for example, is found as a natural preservative in products like cheese, mustard, pepper and yeast.
- "Health food" stores contain many so-called diet foods that differ from other stores' products, only in their exorbitant prices?
- "Low calorie" labeled food can contain no more than 40 calories per serving, and "reduced calorie" products must be 33 percent fewer in calories than the normal product?
- The healthiest five vegetables are collard greens, kale, broccoli, turnip greens and spinach? The healthiest meats are beef liver, chicken liver, liver sausage, chicken breast and tuna? The healthiest fruits include cantaloupe, watermelon, oranges, strawberries and grapefruit?

IS IT TRUE THAT ...
- 90 percent of the fish sold in America has been frozen at one time, and contains too much mercury?
- We shouldn't eat any meat known to have been doped with diethylstilbestrol (DES) or fed antibiotics, hormones, or arsenic-containing feed.
- Sometimes spoiled ice cream is recycled as chocolate so as to cover up the taste?

- Salt, yeast, water and 100 percent stone-ground whole wheat flour should be the only ingredients in bread?
- Homogenized milk is actually unhealthy, and adults don't need milk at all?
- Soft drinks contain ethyl alcohol, acids, BHA, BHT, and as much caffeine as coffee?
- Most anyone with good eating habits has no need to take vitamins?
- Canned vegetables lose 30 percent of their vitamins at the canning plant, 25 percent in the process of sterilization, 27 percent in the discarded liquid, and 12 percent when you heat them?
- You can get almost as much nutrition from sucking on the carton of a T.V. dinner as you can from eating the dinner?
- Some salt companies add sand to their product and label it silicon dioxide?

IS IT TRUE THAT ...
- White bread is allowed to contain plaster of Paris (calcium sulfate)?
- White, refined sugar is not a food but in reality the chemical $C_{12}H_{22}O_{11}$? Also, it contains no vitamins, no useful minerals, no enzymes, no trace elements, no fiber, no protein, no fat, and no benefit whatsoever in the human diet?

Quality eating requires that we look into these things. For your information, you might try a nutrition analysis of your own. Log an average day's consumption.

before breakfast	_____	amount _____
breakfast	_____	amount _____
	_____	amount _____
	_____	amount _____

morning munchies   _____ amount _____

lunch   _____ amount _____

_____ amount _____

_____ amount _____

_____ amount _____

afternoon num-nums   _____ amount _____

supper   _____ amount _____

_____ amount _____

_____ amount _____

_____ amount _____

nighttime naughties   _____ amount _____

Include drinks, bites of other people's food (like half of Tony's candy bar, and the handful of nuts at the office party, etc.) Designate calorie intake, if that is your concern, but the main purpose of this exercise is to examine nutrition. Stare at your summary awhile to spot any outstanding weakness. Are all the food groups there? How much of the food is canned? Pre-packaged? Eaten at a fast food place? Fried?

One book suggests the following as priority foods:

Alfalfa tablets
Avocado
Beans (especially soybeans)
Blackstrap molasses
Brewer's yeast
Breads, 100% whole grain
Carob
Cheeses
Cereal (oats, rice, bran, granola, etc.)
Eggs (a "nearly perfect" food)
Fruit, fresh
Honey
Kefir
Liver

Milk Powder
Nuts
Seeds
Sprouts
Yogurt (especially homemade)

Under foods to go easy on:

Canned fruit
Canned vegetables
Cold cereals
Macaroni
Noodles
Spaghetti
Fat meats

Then come the foods to forget:

Sugar-laden pies, cakes, donuts, cookies
Cola drinks
Processed and precooked frozen dinners
Packaged meats
Coffee
Chocolate
White bread
French fries
Candy
Licorice
Maraschino cherries

(From *How To Eat Right And Feel Great,* by Virginia and Norman Rohrer, Wheaton, Illinois: Tyndale House Publishers, 1977.)

Perhaps quality nutrition isn't your highest priority. However, a few health hints along the way can keep you going longer in whatever kind of living is quality for you. Knowing some general guidelines for keeping the body fit can help you.

Big breakfasts are better than big suppers.
White meat is better than red meat (except liver).
Carob is better than chocolate.
Honey is better than white sugar.
Wheat bread is better than white bread.

Decaffeinated coffee is better than regular coffee.
Herb tea is better than regular tea.
Non-colas are better than colas.
A cheese sandwich is better than packaged meat sandwiches.
Corn tortillas are better than flour tortillas.
Canned fruit in light syrup is better than canned fruit
   in heavy syrup.
Expensive, handpacked ice cream is better than the
   cheap imitation variety.
Cottage cheese is better with a sandwich than french fries.
Meat earlier in the day is better than meat late at night.
Brown rice is better than white rice.
Beans and rice eaten together are better than eaten alone.
Unsweetened yogurt is better than sweetened fruit yogurt.
Fresh veggies are better than frozen, which are better
   than canned.
Fresh fruit is better than fruit pie.
Dry roasted nuts are better than potato chips.
Unsalted sunflower seeds are better than salted nuts.
Potatoes (not fried) are better than noodles.
Vegetable noodles are better than pasta noodles.
Home cooking is better than eating out, which is better
   than T.V. dinners.

You don't need to be a health food fanatic to
grasp quality nutrition. Food seems to bring out ex-
tremes in us all. Either we ignore the whole subject
of nutrition, or we noisily champion its cause. Jesus
said, "For this reason I say to you do not be anxious
for your life, as to what you shall eat, or what you
shall drink; nor for your body, as to what you shall
put on. Is not life more than food, and the body than
clothing?" (Matthew 6:25) Food is important, but
doesn't deserve exclusive concentration.

Two dramatic pictures flash into my mind.

A seventh grade glassmate named Porky lived
back in the age when fat people didn't seem to mind.
He never seemed to complain about the nickname.

We left school that November for the long Thanksgiving weekend, but Porky never returned. He died while eating his Thanksgiving dinner. I never knew the whole story, but maybe his heart couldn't take it. I remember our little band of twelve-year-olds standing around Porky's grave and thinking, "Sure must be more to life than shoveling down food."

Then, there was Carol. At seventeen she had black hair, flashing eyes, and a smile that charmed the toughest teachers. But at 5'3" Carol weighed 83 pounds and she never made it to graduation.

The newspaper headlined the tragic automobile crash. The coroner explained Carol had a kidney failure, and lost consciousness before her blue Mustang went over the bridge.

"She had this phobia about fat," her mother recalled.

Now we call it anorexia.

There has to be more to life than obsessions about food.

And there is.

CHAPTER 8
THE BIG PLUNGE

"He is everything I ever wanted," Melody beamed.

"We met at the Student Leadership Conference. Love at first sight. Like when you see a new dress and something inside you clicks. You just knoiw you're going to buy that dress. That's how it was with Larry.

"And it was the same way for him. He was sitting there in the lobby with his friend, Daren, watching girls. When he saw me he poked Daren and said, 'Hey, that's the one for me!' Really, that's what Daren told me.

"Anyway, Larry lives up on Lakeview Estates. Nice folks. His mother and I get along great. How about that? This last summer Larry and I spent a lot of time together. Did a lot of talking. He really listens, and cares. There's no doubt about it, I've found the right guy."

The more I heard, the more I had to agree with Melody. They married at the beginning of Larry's senior year. Melody got a job in the admissions office of his school. When something happens like that to one of your friends, you're tempted to say, "At least I won't have to worry about this couple."

Wrong again.

New Year's Day I saw Melody at the party, alone. She sounded desperate. "I've got to talk," she said.

We headed for the patio and she spent two hours relating her plight. "That super wedding was the last thing that went right," she began as she choked back the tears. As the story unfolded, I kept waiting for The Big Bomb. Something about the time he came home late, and drunk, and busted her lip. Or maybe he and an old girl friend spent the weekend in Las Vegas. Or, she discovered some perverted sexual demands. But it never came.

Instead, she spilled out a series of unfulfilled expectations. Such as, he didn't carry her over the threshold on their honeymoon because he was embarrassed in front of the people watching. They rarely had breakfast together. He studied late. She worked early. Then, there were Tuesday evenings.

He is never home before 7:00," she complained. "It's his racquetball night."

"Does he ever ask you to join him?" I inquired.

"Sure, all the time, but he knows I hate racquetball. I would gladly play tennis. You know I'm pretty good at that. But, no, Larry can't stand tennis. And he doesn't like Muddles."

"Muddles?"

"My cat. He's always rubbing his nose and faking a sneeze. He claims he's allergic to her. But if he thinks I'm going to get rid of Muddles ... "

On and on ... one little irritation after another.

Melody's dilemma isn't unusual. She suffers from a common misconception about marriage: the perfect mate theory. It goes like this:

Somewhere out there is the absolutely perfect

mate for me. The trick is to find him/her. I will know that a person by an unusual sign (such as a choir of angels singing) that will accompany our meeting. We will marry, and all my needs and desires will be fulfilled by this one.

However,–*if.*

After the marriage, my mate doesn't meet my expectations, *then*, it is because I married the wrong person,

And

My perfect mate is still waiting out there somewhere for me.

There is no such thing as a perfect mate because there is no such thing as a perfect person, yourself included. It is how you deal with and work through imperfections that builds a satisfying marriage, the kind you always wanted to have.

A second mistake is that many intend marriage to be a 50/50 proposition. You do your half, I'll do my half, and it all works out.

But, what happens when your mate goes only 49 percent of the way? Will you dissolve the relationship over a mere 1 percent? If not, would you sometimes be willing to go 51 percent? How about 54 percent? or 60? 75? See what I mean? Marriage must be 100/100. You must be willing to give all it takes all the time. The 50/50 system always breaks down.

A third disastrous misconception is that marriage is like a college major, or a new job. You try it a while, if it doesn't work out, you move on. You can change majors ten times, and vocations every year. But a quality marriage requires the long haul. Commitment is what it's all about.

We all think about marriage. Some are already

married. Some plan to be married in the near future. Some wish they were making wedding plans. Others want nothing to do with the whole thing. But whether you're looking for it, or avoiding it, the subject is usually close at hand.

Chances are, the day will come when a quality marriage relationship will be crucial to your whole lifestyle. Here are ten areas you and your future spouse will need to deal with, in order to achieve satisfaction.

EXPECTATIONS

Like Melody, we all have a picture in our mind of what marriage is like. Maybe it is a picture of a certain house, certain activities, certain attitudes. Maybe for you it is holding hands as you watch the sunset, or candlelight dinners, or sitting in the fifth pew at church. He will teach Junior to play baseball. She will teach Missy to sew, and so forth.

Now, I'm not inferring you must abandon your dream. You must realize that the one you marry has a dream portrait of his own. These dreams often clash. The proper response is to allow these two dreams to gradually, gently merge. You may have to release a few details. The other person may have to, too. The marriage will eventually encompass a total dream, made from separate images that you both bring, and acquire along the way.

With your future/present spouse, describe a typical day you expect in your life together: a) as newlyweds, b) five years later, c) twenty years later. Close your eyes and visualize where you'll be living, what your house looks like, what you'll be doing, what kinds of things you'll own, how your day will begin and end, how close you'll sit to one another in the car, etc. As many details as you can conjure.

ROLES

What is a husband supposed to do? A wife?

Simple questions to reveal signs of role perception. Where do your answers come from? Sometimes from viewing your friends' marriages. Sometimes from what you pick up in the media. Sometimes from books. Many of them come from experiences with Mom and Dad.

Most of us grow up thinking our family situations are the norm. If Mom or Dad exhibit negative characteristics, wea ssume that a good husband/wife will be just the opposite. Either for good or bad, this life encounter shapes your outlook.

Those who join together with differing role model backgrounds will find disagreements. You need to work together to find what fits you best. Your marriage and family won't be just like the one you came from, or the one your partner came from.

Try filling in the following list, then take plenty of time to discuss your answers.

Things a husband should always do:

Things a husband could do if he wanted to:

Things a husband should seldom have to do:

Things a wife could do if she wanted to:

Things a wife should seldom have to do:

IN-LAWS

You inherit the whole gang, not just the one you marry. Some of them you will love, some you will avoid, some you'll never meet, and some you'll never understand. Here are some clues to handling in-laws.

1. *Understand their concern for your fiance(e)/spouse.* They've spent much more time in loving your beloved than you have. They've charted the future, wanting (from their viewpoint) only the best. They've made mistakes, but they do care. Allow them to show concern, even if at times it seems to interfere.

2. *Compliment your fiance(e)/spouse in your in-law's presence.* They want the assurance that you truly love and respect their child. Words as well as actions count here. Seeing the two of you snuggle and kiss is nice, but that could mean you're only interested in sex. They want to hear what you think as well.

3. *Don't push yourself to outdo them.* Don't try to outcook your mother-in-law or out-golf your father-in-law unless this comes without unnatural effort. You do not have to compete with them for your lover's attention; you're on a completely different level.

4. *Be yourself.* Try to overcome the initial discomfort quickly, and fit into the family the best you can. Don't begin by trying to be someone you're not. It is hard to keep up in the years ahead.

5. *Work at developing a mutual interest.* If your future in-laws seem to exist in a different world, watch for something you can both agree upon. Hobbies, sports, politics, crafts, anything. It insures a conversation starter and enjoyable visits.

6. *Be fair with your time.* How often do you visit your folks? How often with the in-laws? Sometimes, due to distance or schedules, one set of parents be-

come the most often visited. But be sensitive to feelings. If one family thinks they're being slighted, try within reason to make amends.

7. *Avoid family comparisons.* It is not always a matter of right or wrong, but of traditions and environment. Enjoy the uniqueness of each family.

8. *Be friendly, but not too familiar.* You might come from a hugging family, kisses and pats for everyone. If that is foreign to your in-laws, be sensitive. Observe the family's customs of conduct.

9. *Treat them as they should be, not as they might deserve to be treated.* So the brother's a jerk—treat him with as much respect as you can muster. Families tend to see the best in their members, especially when threatened by "outsiders."

10. *Talk openly with your fiance(e)/spouse when you're having trouble with the in-laws.* Don't hide it. Demonstrate an open attitude of wanting to work things out.

QUARRELS

Fights and arguments are a natural process for any two people who honestly work to build a lasting relationship. The question is not, do you ever argue? Rather, how do you argue? The way you solve small differences affects your approach to the larger ones. Here are some suggestions for having a "good" fight.

1. *Handle differences as soon as possible.* The Bible says, "Don't let the sun go down on your anger" (Eph. 4:26). Don't go to sleep until you've gotten the thing off your chest. Talk it out to an understanding or solution.

2. *Forget the past.* Every time you bring up some

past mistake, past relationship or past experience, you demonstrate lack of concrete evidence for the present situation. In a courtroom, the defendant's past isn't allowed as evidence if the case is open and shut ... and you're not in a courtroom.

3. *Keep arguments in perspective.* How important is the matter anyway? In the total picture of your long-term commitment, how crucial is this? Keep it in balance.

4. *Look for deeper causes.* Sometimes the minor items of an argument reflect a deeper habit or characteristic that is really the issue. Dig for this. Patching up constant feuds without correcting the main sore spot is wearisome work.

5. *Don't run away.* Stick in there, eyeball to eyeball, big toe to big toe, until you both understand, and agree to a course of action.

6. *Realize your differences in perspective.* A little thing to one can be a big deal to another. You both may be right. Attempt to see the problem from the other viewpoint, too.

PROMISES

Keep them. Keep them all. Never underestimate the importance of backing your words with action, on even the most trivial matters. Your test in being trusted for important promises begins with smaller situations. Don't give room for your integrity to be doubted.

If you say you'll be there by 6:00, don't accept 6:20, or 7:00, or tomorrow. Always let the other person know why if you must break a promise. If you said you'd go shopping on Saturday, refuse the baseball tickets given to you at the last moment. If you said you would mend the torn shirt, don't watch the soap opera instead.

Don't make a promise you know you won't keep. Keep every promise you make. It is as simple as that. It will be the glue that holds your relationsip together in the most trying of times.

DECISIONS

Who decides what kind of car to buy? Which style of furniture? How much to spend on the T.V. set? When to spank the kids? When to move? Who decides on wardrobes? And careers? Are all decisions 50/50?

What happens when you disagree? I conversed recently with some friends who have been married twelve years. He still thinks she should accept, without question, his logic: "Because that's the way I want to do it."

Take time to explain your position. Postpone any major decisions until there is mutual agreement. It is surprising how many things can wait. Make your own ground rules for handling conflicts before they come, then stick with them during the battle.

MONEY

A common subject of contention. What do you do when you don't have enough? What do you do with the extra? What do you purchase? And why? What happens to it? Why can't you afford it? A quality financial game plan will minimize the struggles. Here is what it should include:

First, agree upon a budget. (See Chapter 4.) A budget can be changed, or amplified as you go along, but it is a target to begin with. The budget should reflect both your desires, and support both your dreams, if possible. Make one out yearly, monthly, or weekly. The more you strive to agree before the money is spent, the less hassle later.

Second, break the habit of believing there is a direct correlation between fun and money.

"What do you want to do for fun tonight?"

"We can't, we're broke."

This leads to resenting not having money, as well as despising the items on which you spend it. And a warped view of contentment results.

Third, consider it "our money." No matter who hauls in the income, it is all "ours," instead of "yours" and "mine." That doesn't mean you can't allot some cash to each other that remains unaccounted for. And you allow for those unexpected odds and ends, for saving, for whatever. But, the mindset remains: We are in this financial partnership together.

Fourth, set limits. Determine how much money can be spent from your joint account without your partner's prior approval. It is your decision. That way you know the rules if you happen onto a perfect shirt or blouse during your lunch break. It avoids unpleasant surprises that often lead to knockdown dragouts.

Fifth, include the important things. For instance, prepare for the future with insurance policies, savings accounts, and retirement plans. Include priorities such as yearly vacations, nights on the town, hobbies, and continuing education. They can be integral to quality living.

CHANGES

There won't be many.

There will be many.

Both statements are true. Don't assume everything will be perfect as soon as your partner changes. And don't make the mistake of believing you're just the one to straighten him/her out. You probably won't. Commit yourself to him/her without conditions. Even if no changes are ever made, this is the one you would like to spend a lifetime with.

Now, changes do occur. Years of living and loving make you more and more like each other. Rough spots do smooth over. Habits do alter. It is possible to grow in love. But, you can't count on these changes to make the relationship tolerable. Accept the faults from the start, without reservations, or don't get involved at all.

SEX

This source of friction is second only to money. Some things to remember:

Men are different from women. What might be a fulfilling sexual expression for one, isn't for the other. You need to talk about it. It is crucial in this area to give pleasure as well as to receive.

You probably don't know very much about sex. Oh, I know, you've read manuals, viewed films, talked a lot, maybe experimented, etc. But, that doesn't mean too much in a lifetime partnership. Sex in general doesn't translate well to sex in specific. How to give one unique, individual, special person true sexual satisfaction takes years of practice.

You've got to be a better lover five years from

now, than you are now.

Don't accept everything you hear about sexual behavior. Nothing is worse than to base your relationship on: "Well, I read that most men ... " or "My sister said I should never ... " or "Why can't you be like ... " or "It looked good on the centerfold model... "

God gave the pleasures of sex as a gift to couples committed to each other. How often? Whenever you both want to. Where? Anywhere that is private. How? Any way you both enjoy.

FAITH

I hold two basic assumptions about marriage.

First, God desires that everyone who chooses to marry will have an enjoyable, fulfilling relationship. It may take the entire lifetime to build and perfect the finer points, but the marriage will bloom.

Second, a good, quality marriage comes by establishment of godly, biblical principles. Now, I know of good marriages where the couple appears to have no visible faith in God, no attention to Scriptures, and no commitment to a church. But, all of these relationships are held together by principles learned from and accepted by another person where such faith was important.

So, Mom and Dad have a great marriage without a personal relationship with God. But where did they learn those characteristics of loyalty, integrity and self-sacrifice? Probably from Grandma and Grandpa. Remember them? The gray-haired couple who always went to church (maybe took you along when you were a kid). They said prayers at the dinner table, and displayed the big black book on the coffee table. Avoiding biblical principles can cost you quality.

110

Trusting in God's way solves a number of problems within a marriage. It is no longer only your way, or your mate's way, but rather, "Let's find God's way." Some day it will all hit you. Marriage, then maybe raising children. Suddenly, you panic. How to handle the task, the responsibility!

A couple who grows in their mutual understanding of God, and discovers His best guidance for their lives, has a three-mile headstarts over all others seeking a quality marriage.

A final word on one of the fun parts of marriage, the wedding service itself. Aim for quality there, too.

Get married in a church because you want everyone to know that your commitment goes beyond social amenities. It is an agreement witnessed by God.

Invite lots of people. You want the whole world to know about your love for each other.

Make the day memorable. It is a big deal, so let loose.

But, make it reasonable. Watch the expense. People won't be favorably impressed with the money you spend. They'll note how happy you seem, and how the ceremony uniquely expresses who you are.

Make it respectful. Respect the wishes of both families. Respect God's house. Respect your guests.

Make it serious. Choose music that reflects your statement of love. Repeat vows that reveal the depth of your love and commitment.

Make it fun. A Super Bowl game can be both fun and serious. So can a wedding and marriage. Don't allow outside pressures to ruin your day. The ringbearer may fall asleep. Uncle Waldo may show up drunk. You may forget a line. If you get tired of all that picture-taking, ask the photographer to excuse you. It is your day; you're in charge. Let those days, weeks, and months of expectation burst into smiles and contentment.

Quality married life ... it is hard to be a loser if you've got that.

Chapter 9
Is There Life Without Panic?

"Go away!" Kathy's shout could be heard down the hall and through the lobby. It was close to 10:30 P.M. when Mandy stopped by to see if Kathy would stop for a coffee break.

Why the scream? Because Kathy's term paper sat half finished in her typewriter. Only four pages in two and a half hours.

At 8:10 Kathy's roommate, Beth, insisted she go down to meet her brother, who had stopped by on his way to Hawaii. At 8:35 she received a phone call from home. Mom wanted to know why she hadn't written Gram lately. At 9:00 several girls on the floor wanted to use Kathy's T.V. to watch the evening sports news. They thought the camera had scanned them in the crowd in the basketball game coverage.

At 9:20 she discovered the toilet overflowing, and had to find someone to fix it. Then at 10:05 the quotation mark key on her typewriter stuck. At 10:24 she discovered she had turned the carbon paper backwards on page 13. It would have to be typed over again. Then, at 10:30, along comes Mandy.

Stress.

Endless interruptions.

It happens to people other than dorm dwellers, too.

If you work hard enough, you can get ahead. That is what Tim always believed. Now, he isn't sure. That philosophy had helped him sail through college, even with juggling a job after school and weekends.

Then began the long grind of commuting to the downtown Houston corporate offices of one of the nation's leading banks. He started at the bottom, but there was plenty of upward mobility. He used his vacations for further training: enrolled in an accelerated MBA nightschool program, joined several influential service clubs, and brought home a loaded briefcase every Friday night. Now, the payoff. Rumors circulated that twenty-eight-year-old Tim would be moving upstairs.

Tim wondered just how far upstairs. Every day about 2:00 P.M. a dull, throbbing headache set in. Lately, he had noticed an occasional cramp in his left chest.

Stress.

Activity overload.

"How could I have forgotten!" Paul couldn't believe it. Friday night the whole family gathered to celebrate Dad's birthday. The big 60. Paul's Mom had called his apartment. No answer. He was sitting in the local theater viewing a 1952 Gary Cooper classic. It wasn't that important. He could have gone some other day. But, what a hectic week.

His car had been at the garage, so he bummed rides to work. He'd forgotten to return the rented tux. Five days late. Thursday morning Lance showed up to stay a few days. Friday, Paul ran all over town trying to find size 5 black shoes for his boss' wife. Finally, the week over, he picked up his car and stopped by the cleaners, and that was when he noticed the ad for "High Noon." Frank Miller hit the dust, and Paul remembered the birthday party! He arrived, gift in hand, just as Aunt Sophia and the others were leaving.

Stress.

Inadequate organization.

Pamela looked worried. She should have been. After fifteen weeks and forty-five class hours, she still didn't know much about the history of 16th Century English Literature. She had attended most of the classes, but hadn't taken many notes. Her roommate took the class last year, and had a meticulous set of systematic notes. Pamela planned to review those. She kept saying she would set aside a whole weekend just to study those notes, but it didn't happen.

She determined to make this her Thanksgiving vacation project, but it snowed. She couldn't miss the first skiing of the year. So here it was, the day before finals. The library was crowded and noisy. She could only skim the roommate's notes. She never finished reading the chapters. She was sure she would flunk the course, and her grade point average would drop. She feels a real crying spell coming on.

Stress.

Procrastination.

Time magazine quotes Dr. Hans Selye, the Austrian-born founding father of stress research. He defines stress as "the rate of wear and tear in the body" (June 6, 1983, page 49). We all understand this. Stress has become an accepted part of everydy

American existence.

To your doctor stress looks like this:

The emotional pressure causes the brain to send chemical messages to the hypothalamus, which causes production of a chemical called CRF. Part of the CRF is converted by the pituitary to the hormone ACTH, which travels through the bloodstream and reaches the outside layer of the adrenal glands, thus initiating the production of cortisone which in turn increases the blood sugar and speeds up the body's metabolism. The CRF also triggers the electrochemical impulses down to the brain stem and spinal cord and reaches the core of the adrenal glands. Epinephrine and norepinephrine are released, which supply extra glucose, speed up the heartbeat and raise blood pressure.

That is what stress looks like to your doctor. To you and me, it means stomach aches, migraines, short tempers, and a desire to run away from it all. How big a problem is it? Stress is known to be a major contributor, either directly or indirectly, to coronary heart disease, cancer, lung ailments, accidental injuries, cirrhosis of the liver, and suicide. These are the leading causes of death in the United States. Stress isn't limited to corporate executives, or busy professionals. It has become one of the chief problems facing eighteen-to-twenty-year-olds as well.

CHANGE

Change is one of the chief promoters of stress. You've probably seen the Holmes-Rahe Social Readjustment Rating Scale. Listed in degree of seriousness are such things as: death of a close family member, personal injury or illness, marriage, losing your job, pregnancy, death of a close friend, switching jobs, change in responsibilities on the job, outstanding personal achievment, beginning or ending school, altered living conditions, revision of personal habits, switch in work hours. Any change of residence, schools, sleeping habits, eating habits, and even vacations can cause stress (*Journal Of Psychosomatic Research*, Elmsford, N.Y.: Pergamon Press, Ltd., 1967, 2:216, table III).

Any of the first half-dozen stress producers can have major effects. Yet if we find ourselves with several of the minor producers, the cumulative consequence can be as great.

There are other conditions, besides change, that produce stress.

AUTHORITATIVENESS

Jim is the eldest of six children. He was the high school class valedictorian and president of the Southwest Student League. Now, at twenty-six, he manages a department store in a fashionable West Los Angeles shopping center. If you want to get a job done right, ask Jim. There is only one way to do anything, and that is Jim's way. He dominates groups, dictates decisions, overpowers relationships, and chews chalky white pills to settle his stomach.

Authoritativeness is characterized by one who favors absolute obedience and sovereign rule, as opposed to individual freedom. Test yourself.

_____ Do you find it difficult, if not impossible, to find competent co-workers?

_____ Would you rather do a job correctly yourself,

117

than take time to show someone else how to do it?

_____ When working on a project with others, do you feel as though you must supervise every aspect?

INTOLERANCE

Kristie wants another biology lab partner. Marjolein, her current partner, gagged her way through frog dissection, and refuses to cut into the piglet. "I find it incredible, that someone twenty years old can't sit still for ninety minutes to examine pickled pig!" Kristie fumes.

On the other hand, Kristie can't figure out why anyone would want to live in a high-rise urban apartment, own a Japanese car, eat yogurt, or root for any other team but the Green Bay Packers.

Intolerance includes failure to allow or respect the nature, beliefs, or behavior of others.

_____ Do you get impatient when others around you waste time and don't get right to the point?

_____ Do you assume that there is one right way of doing things, and once that is discovered, there is no further discussion needed?

_____ Do you find yourself, your attitudes, and your actions to be the standard by which everyone else is measured?

IDEALISM

Jenny is almost 30. This fall begins her seventh year teaching fifth graders. She enjoys teaching, but it is not her primary interest. What she wants more than anything is to get married and raise a family. She has just the guy in mind. He is tall, tanned and has strong arms. He is sensitive, loving and gentle.

Not only that, but he is open, adventurous, and fun to be around. She just can't seem to find anyone who fits his mental image.

Idealism means being over concerned with what "should be," rather than with what "is." It can be transferred to people, or places, or environments.

_____ Do most products and people fail to live up to your expectations?

_____ Do you find yourself saying often, "This just shouldn't be happening to me!"?

_____ Do you find your plans seem reasonable and complete, until you put them into practice, and then they seldom come out as you anticipated?

INDECISIVENESS

Derrick wants to get into the computer field. He thinks. He is twenty-five and has just finished junior college. He took six years to complete a two-year course. Well, there was the spring he took a leave, and thought about getting a job. However, he never found the right one.

He changed from an ag major to poly sci, then converted to geography. At one time he considered art and music, but lost interest when he entered the theory classes. He spent one winter in a mountain cabin writing a book, but now, he is almost sure it is computers. If only he can decide which school to attend.

Indecisiveness produces constant hesitation, lack of certainty, vacillation about making choices. At times, it happens to us all. For some, it is a way of life.

_____ Does fear of making a wrong decision dominate your mind while facing tough choices?

_____ Are you more comfortable when other people tell you what to do?

_____ Are there some problems you face that just seem to drag on and on with no solution in sight?

PERFECTIONISM

Mark wrote a few poems for a campus literary publication. He received much praise for his work. A national college magazine spied them, and wrote for permission to reprint one of the poems. He asked for time to give it a little more polish, since it would be getting that much attention. They agreed to wait. That was a year and a half ago. Mark works on the poem every once in awhile. But, it is never quite right.

Perfectionism, in the negative sense, is that inordinate desire to make everything, and everyone, flawless. It is pushing ahead to highest excellence. No defects.

_____ Can you name three projects (or more) that have been waiting for you to find time to finish them?

_____ Do you find it hard to find anyone who can do a job the way it ought to be done?

_____ Do you get upset easily when others ignore details?

REPRESSION

You would never know it to look at him. Boisterous, always smiling, life-of-the-party Eddie Gant. Who would guess that out of the graduating class of '79, he'd be the most likely to commit suicide? Oh, it hasn't happened ... yet. But, Eddie has never gotten over the fact that Liz went away to college and married a pilot.

Then, there was the wreck on the Interstate. It wasn't Eddie's fault at all, but two little kids were killed. After that, the foulup with the phone company, his boss who is constantly on his case, and the guy who conned him out of $2,500. If the truth were known, Eddie's downward cycle began when his Dad was shot down over Viet Nam. Missing In Action, they still claim.

Repression is the holding in of hurts. It is the stockpiling of agony. It is clinging to pain when you need to let it out.

_____ Can you name two close friends with whom you could share almost anything?

_____ Would you say that you constantly (once a week or more) dwell on an event or action of the distant past?

_____ Do you believe others would be shocked if they knew how you really felt?

AMPLIFICATION

"Why do things like this always happen to me?" Maggie blasted at her roommates. "Everything goes all right for you, but I had to spend thirty-five minutes looking for that new lipstick. By the time I got to work, all the parking places were taken. I had to walk four blocks. Four blocks!

"I busted the heel off my shoe," she continued. "Then, we had this temporary helper in the office. She was a pain. She showed up at the title company wearing a low-cut, bright green dress. The guys acted like jerks."

Then, "Hey, did you know Luigi's is closed for remodeling? I didn't know, so I walked all the way down there at lunch. And you wouldn't believe the traffic tonight. It is like playing roller derby in a car."

And, "I thought you were going to clean up the dishes. Are those last night's dishes? Didn't you hear me this morning? I guess I'll have to ... Are you listening?"

Amplification—magnification of minor irritants and annoyances beyond their importance or significance.

_____ Are you surprised to have a good day, one when most everything goes right?

_____ Do others usually think less of your problems than you do, and not seem to care what you're going through?

_____ Do you find it easy to jot down a list of "pet peeves?"

UNCOMMUNICATIVENESS

Ask Andy how things are going. The answer is always the same. "Perfect, everything is just perfect."

His Dad could have died, his parakeet flown out the window, his car crashed, or his angel food cake fallen, but he would never let on. Many of us are that way.

"How are you?" doesn't mean you really want to know. And, the reply, "I'm doing fine," says nothing about what you're really going through. Such conversation signifies nothing more than "I recognize you as another human being," and "Okay, I'll recognize you as well."

Being uncommunicative ... the failure to communicate your true feelings.

_____ Do you feel like no one knows the real you?

_____ Do you feel that every time you reveal something personal, people misinterpret what you say?

_____ Do you feel that if people really knew you, they'd change their opinion of you?

FATALISM

"Someone is out to get me," Denny complained to the others in the locker room. "I can't save any money, because it takes every penny to fix up my old car. I can't get rid of the car because it was my grandpa's. Grandma gave it to me when he died."

"Denny, how come you didn't tackle that tight end?"

"I tripped on the lousy seam of that Astroturf. Ask Lourey, he saw it."

"You did stumble around out there," Lourey interjected.

"Yeah, I never can get on top of things."

Fatalism is the belief that there are forces outside your control dictating your actions and feelings.

_____ Do you always feel about one step shy of getting free from outside influences?

_____ Do you find yourself excusing your actions by exclaiming, "That's just the way I am?"

_____ Do you figure your habits and responses to situations are well entrenched, that is useless to try to change them?

NEED OF APPROVAL

Marcy has always tried hard to please. If someone at work mentions she doesn't like the color of Marcy's blouse, she never wears it again. If Mom hints that she ought to come home for the weekend, Marcy drops everything and returns. She was upset for three days because a stranger honked at her and yelled something about her driving.

She breaks into tears over a scowl. She is depressed for days if a friend fails to call. If you want Marcy to go bowling, she'll go. If you ask her to stay home, she'll stay. Nice, quiet, peaceful Marcy. No one knows about the knot in her stomach.

Marcy has the need to seek love and approval from everyone at all times.

_____ Do you spend more time thinking about what others think of you than completing the task at hand?

_____ Do you constantly feel overshadowed by the popularity of those around you?

_____ Do you find it hard to go on when you discover someone, anyone, is opposed to your actions?

So you have discovered stress in your life. What do you do now? Far more important than searching for a hassle-free existence, is finding quality. That is, discovering your manageable level of stress, the level that propels, rather than crushes, your activity. Stress can be managed by dealing with it on three levels.

Your Body

1. Get in shape. Good health aids survival in a high-stress position. This includes eyesight, hearing and teeth as well as heart, lungs and kidneys.

2. Achieve the appropriate weight for your height. Your doctor can advise in this area. However, as you work on getting your weight down, don't allow this to cause additional stress. Pick out a slow, gradual, sensible weight-loss plan. Take all the time you need. Accept any progress as victory, and tolerate the fat on the way to thin.

3. *Eat at least one hot, well-balanced meal a day, home-cooked, if possible.* Relax while eating. This meal should not be at the office, in the car, or in front of the T.V.

4. *Insist on seven to eight hours of sleep, five nights a week.* The quality of your waking hours often depends on the quantity of your sleeping hours.

5. *Exercise to the point of heavy perspiration at least twice a week.* Run, dance, work out, play rugby, lift weights, or attempt a triathalon. It is needed to tone the muscles, build up the heart, and strengthen the lungs.

6. *Eliminate obvious poisons.* If you can't avoid them altogether, cut down. This includes drugs, cigarettes, alcohol and caffein.

7. *Take short physical breaks during stress times.* Deep sighs do wonders for tense bodies.

Your Mind

1. *Clarify job duties and role expectations, job descriptions, house rules, friendship responsibilities.* Knowing all these can help eliminate stress.

2. *Receive and give affection.* Kiss your mother, hug the cat, and tell a friend how much he means to you. Accept the offered affections of others as well.

3. *Live within fifty miles of a relative upon whom you can really count.* A one-hour drive to see the folks, a brother, or good old Uncle Percy, can reinforce the fact that you are not an emotional island alone on a hostile planet.

4. *Establish an adequate income to meet basic expenses.* If this requires more training, then go for it.

If it means moving, then move. Financial worries over basics keep many in continual stress.

5. *Join and regularly support a social group or club.* Make it fun. Make it something you truly enjoy. Make it a habit. It can force you into a different environment, open up new abilities in you, and create new friendships.

6. *Develop a network of close friends.* (See Chapter 2.) Appoint yourself chief initiator of activities, and take the lead in being your open, honest self when you get together with "your gang."

7. *Develop one or two closer friends, with whom you are free to share the most personal matters.* Work at building and maintaining these friendships. Meet with these people on a regular basis, in an environment that allows private conversation.

8. *Speak honestly about your feelings when you are hurt, angry or worried.* Be fair, tactful, courteous and gentle, but don't hold it all in.

9. *Organize your time.* It is not necessary to account for every minute, but chart a general calendar, and stick to it. You'll get more done and be less anxious about the future.

10. *Discuss common matters and problems often with the people with whom you live.* How is the money holding out? Are the chores getting done to evryone's satisfaction? What changes need to be made?

11. *Find some private time every day.* (See Chapter 3.) Close the closet door, go for a walk, get to your office early (if it is empty), or sit out on a balcony and stare at the stars.

12. *Do something just for fun once a week.* It is not a luxury, but a necessity. All work and no play gives

Jack perforated ulcers, a weak heart and a lousy disposition.

YOUR SPIRIT

Perhaps you've never considered the stress your spiritual life, or lack of it, causes you. Take the following True/False test.

_____ What I say I believe about spiritual matters and what I really believe are two different things.

_____ I handle thoughts about my own death by banishing them from my mind.

_____ I view reliance upon spiritual help as irrational and a sign of weakness.

_____ Even if I wanted to investigate spiritual truth, it is too late for me now.

_____ Spiritual truth is not relevant to the real world in which I live.

_____ I know what I ought to do about my spiritual life, but I can't bring myself to do it.

_____ I tried religion (praying, going to church) once, and it did not seem to do any good.

_____ I would not consider talk about the spiritual realm worthwhile except for the personal experiences of some trusted people I know.

_____ I would rather others did not know of my interest in exploring spiritual truth.

_____ Even if I were interested in the spiritual world, I would not know where to begin.

The more _True_ answers you have marked, the more you are experiencing stress caused by spiritual conflicts. Life goes on, even in the most stressful of times, and quality living can help resolve much of that stress.

The next three chapters will show some practical, effective ways to deal with spiritual needs.

Chapter 10
What If
The Elevator Cable Snaps?

How would you like to discuss something ugly?
Like dying, or death?

Neither would I.

So, let's forget the subject, and move on. Put it into the category of "One of those things I should consider some day." Plan for the future. Enjoy today. Think good, positive thoughts, and maybe ...

It is no use. Sooner or later it catches up.

Barry got a call in the middle of the night from his mom. She phoned from the emergency room at the hospital. Something about dad's heart. When Barry rushed through the doors of County General, his dad was prepped and being wheeled into the operating room. Ruptured aorta, the nurse said. Barry and his mother settled in for the long night in the intensive care unit waiting room. They didn't have to wait long. Forty-seven minutes later the doctors announced that Barry's dad was dead.

Barry suddenly realized that some things were up to him now. His mother needed comfort. All he could offer was bitterness and anger. His dad was only fifty-one. Too young to leave them ... no more deer-hunting trips, no more Monday night football, no more fixing the water pump, no more security in just knowing he is there, no more jokes about Barry's hair, no more brown khaki work pants, no more counselor and friend. Ugly .

Evie was startled to see her brother walking toward her in the university library. She knew something must be wrong. Lyle lived over an hour away. She hadn't seen him in months.

"It's little Luke. He fell into a pool. It doesn't look good ... "

As she hurried along with Lyle, Evie thought about her nephew. Only eighteen months old, and just starting to run and climb. The first grandchild. The star at every family gathering.

"He's just got to make it," Evie pleaded.

The hallway was jammed with relatives when they arrived. Premature, sick babies cried at every window. Right now, only one mattered to Evie. Hours ticked by. Days came and went. A week passed. Evie forgot about class, grades, homework. On the 11th day, little Luke died. Evie cried all night. That was four years ago. Every time she thinks about it, she still cries. Very Ugly .

They both knew the heavy rain made the roads slick and dangerous. Ben alone knew that the front tires on the import were really bad. "We'll be all right as long as I have no sudden stops," he thought.

Then, Carol shrieked. An old black pickup loomed toward them. Wild spinning out of control. Explosions, panic, and pain. Ben woke up to bright lights, both legs in casts, and sharp pain in his ribs.

"How's Carol?" he managed to ask.

The young nurse turned her head. The doctor spoke. "I'm afraid she's dead."

Ben hardly felt the needle of the sedative. "Oh, God, no!" he cried as the horror washed over him.

Ben sat in a wheel chair when they lowered Carol into the grave. Ben, and about five hundred others, crowded around the Sunnyside Memorial Park Cemetery site.

The casts are off now. But, you don't see Ben around much any more. Keeps to himself. Never dates. Some things take time. A long time. Very, very ugly.

There is hardly a human that hasn't stood at a grave and demanded, "Why?" Why do we have to die? It doesn't seem right. It isn't natural. It isn't fair. The more we try to hide from it, the greater the shock when it comes.

People die.

To be more specific, mothers die, fathers die, babies die, and girlfriends and boyfriends die.

Even more specifically, you will die and so will I.

Since it is a guaranteed experience for each of us, it is understandable that we want to know why.

The medical and legal professions have had a hard time defining death. They tell us it probably happens when the brain waves cease. They can tell us when it occurs and how, and with careful examination, what the probable cause was. They may be able to tell us how to prevent a similar thing from happening to us.

131

But there is one thing they never discuss: Why?

Where do you go to find answers about death? New books are being written every day. Sensational stories explode from magazine headlines. But the statements conflict. How do you know which sources to trust? Here are six questions worth asking anyone who claims to have knowledge about death, and afterdeath.

1. Has this source been around long enough to stand the test of many generations? Any person, coherent or incoherent, sober or drunk, sane or insane, can claim some revelation. But truth isn't a fad. Truth seldom gets good press coverage. Truth isn't that exciting to talk about at the hairdressers. But truth endures. Right through the global conflicts and petty family squabbles. Through centuries and cynicism, it remains.

2. Does the source rely on more than one person's opinion? While some truth has first been discovered, or formulated, by one person, it makes sense to many others around him. In fact, others often take this information and with further investigation add new insights to the truth themselves. If the main source of information about death, and the life hereafter, comes from one individual, and if that information is so distant and complicated that it is truly understood only by the founder, then there is reason to doubt.

3. Does the source address the problem directly? What is said about the real questions? Does it help where you hurt? Or does it merely hint at solutions, or even worse, does it seem to treat lightly the very matters that trouble you most?

A book on typewriter repair that jokes about the "Grand word processor in the sky" hardly qualifies as a stable source. Neither does a philosophy book on the history of theological ideas.

4. Has the source proven to be reliable in other areas? You believe new truth that comes from people who've proven themselves trustworthy concerning other subjects. They've not given you reason to doubt their sincerity. You buy *How To Cook The World's Best Lasagna* cookbook from the same publisher that printed your old favorite, *How To Cook The World's Best Hot Dogs.* You figure if they're so accurate in one area, you can trust them in another.

5. Is the source based on some objective fact? Does it tie into history? Is there anything in your experience, or those of others around you, that would tend to confirm this claim?

6. Has this source proven itself to be of positive value and help to others? What happens when reliable people accept this information? How does it affect their lives? If it remains merely trivia in the periphery of their minds, it may not be that important to investigate. If it transforms their thinking, and drives them on to sacrificial acts, check into its validity.

Death, dying, and afterlife ... where do you turn for answers? Let me suggest the Bible. Applying the preceding questions, let's see how it rates.

QUESTION #1: Yes, the Bible has withstood the test of time. It remains the world's #1 best seller. It has been an inspiration to mideastern tribesmen, sophisticated Roman citizens, recluse monks, Renaissance men, and people of nearly every race, tongue and culture. It transcends economics, politics, and social structures.

QUESTION #2: Yes, the Bible was written over a

2,000-year period of history, by at least forty-one different authors. Yet, the unity of thought is incredible. It stands, not as the belief of only forty-one people, but of millions upon millions of folks who have found its truth authentic in their own lives.

QUESTION #3: Yes, the Bible is all about living, dying, and living again. The first few chapters describe why man dies, and the last few chapters handle what happens after death. The pages in between complete the picture.

QUESTION #4: Yes, the Bible's wisdom covers the subjects of family relationships, handling forgivness, dealing with priorities, helping the needy, living a fulfilling life, to mention a few. This insight has sustained generations of believers. Its historical accuracy has never been successfully challenged. It remains the Book of all books.

QUESTION #5: Yes, the Bible is based on objective facts. For instance, the resurrection of Jesus Christ. Here is an event that would have been most advantageous for both the Roman and Jewish authorities to disprove, yet they were unable to do it. He appeared not only to His disciples and friends, but also to "more than five hundred people at one time" (1 Corinthians 15:6, LB).

QUESTION #6: Yes, the positive value of the Bible in the lives of others is all around us. The apostles of Jesus Christ, who hid in fear after His death, suddenly became fearless, ready to cast themselves to the lions, if necessary, after they claimed His resurrection. You probably know people, right in your own family, who right now enjoy peace and freedom from the fear of death, a peace and freedom that you envy.

Am I saying that the Bible is the only source of truth about death, dying, and afterlife? Not yet. That is something everyone must discover for themselves. What I am saying is that it is definitely one reliable source, and for that reason cannot be ignored.

Here are the Bible's answers to a few of the most-asked questions about death and life after death.

WHY IS THERE PHYSICAL SUFFERING?

In the creation account of the first two chapters of Genesis, the world existed without suffering. The first man, Adam, and the first woman, Eve, knew joy, delight, security and satisfaction. While there is no mention of suffering, there is talk of obedience. A minor stipulation was made. Everything was theirs to enjoy, except for the fruit of one single tree.

As most of us know, they flunked the test. In doing so, they rejected God's control and His wisdom, and they attempted to usurp His position. The punishment, of which they were warned ahead of time, is just. The events that follow are not due to God's creation, but man's disobedience and perversion of that creation. The freedom to twist His creation into a suffering world was one of the choices allotted to mankind by God.

A related question often asked is, "why do good people suffer?"

There is, in the question, the assumption that being good frees one from the curse of a messed up creation. We're all stuck on the same out-of-whack planet. Another assumption is, a certain degree of "goodness" should exempt you from suffering. That isn't the Bible's view. (More about that in Chapter 11.)

WHY DO PEOPLE DIE?

Every grieving person wonders. There is something absurd about death. Something deep and primal inside us protests that it just shouldn't be.

Man was not created to die. The Bible says we were created to know God. "And this is eternal life, that they may know Thee, the only true God, and Jesus Christ whom Thou has sent" (John 17:3, NASB). But how can dead people know God? If mankind was created to enjoy friendship with God, what happened?

Genesis 2 explains that man's rebellion against God and rejection of His rule brought death into our world. "And the Lord God commanded the man, saying, 'From any tree of the garden you may eat freely; but from the tree of knowledge of good and evil you shall not eat, for in the day that you eat from it you shall surely die.'"

So, one man's action brought death to us all. The Bible also states that "Yes, all have sinned; all fall short of God's glorious ideal" (Romans 3:23, LB).

A natural question that next arises: Why did God create a world, and a creature that could get so messed up? Because he wanted people who would voluntarily choose to love and acknolwedge Him. Not just robots. Death is not natural, but it is logical—the reasonable culmination for mankind's rebellion.

WHAT HAPPENS AT THE POINT OF DEATH?

I'll leave to the scientists and physicians the data concerning the physical phenomenon. But, what happens spiritually? According to the Bible each of us is created with both a body and a soul (Genesis 2:7). At death there is a separation of the body and soul (or spirit) (Ecclesiastes 12:7).

A spirit is hard to define. No autopsy ever revealed one. Yet, there's something about you that makes you who you are, apart from the physical. You can lose a limb, have a transplant, receive a transfusion, and you're still you. The spirit is your essence.

There is no argument about what happens to the body. We all know it is placed in the ground, scattered at sea, or whatever. But the spirit or soul, leaves the body. For some, they enter into Christ's presence. Jesus said this to a thief who came to believe in Him as the two hung dying on Roman crosses, "Today you will be with Me in Paradise. This is a solemn promise" (Luke 23:43).

IS THERE REALLY LIFE AFTER DEATH?

The bookstores are filled with sensational accounts of hospital deaths. The people are revived and tell about their spiritual experiences. However, most of these accounts bring confusion, and have limited value. Seldom do they meet the prerequisites for establishing truth as mentioned earlier.

One can, as many do, reject Christianity in its entirety. But, it is impossible to accept some of the tenets of Christ, and reject the idea of life after death. It is the central core of all He taught. Paul expressed it this way,

> For if there is no resurrection of the dead, then Christ must still be dead. And if He is still dead, then all our preaching is useless and your trust in God is empty, worthless, hopeless; and we apostles are all liars because we have said that God raised Christ from the grave, and of course that isn't true if the dead do not come back to life again. If they don't then Christ is still dead, and you are very foolish to keep on trusting

137

God to save you, and you are still under condemnation for your sins; in that case all Christians who have died are lost! And if being a Christian is of value to us only now in this life, we are the most miserable of creatures" (1 Corinthians 15:13-19, LB).

Life after death is the foundational truth of Christianity. Paul immediately reassures the Corinthians that "the fact is that Christ did actually rise from the dead, and has become the first of millions who will come back to life again some day" (1 Corinthians 15:20, LB).

Jesus stated, "I say emphatically that anyone who listens to My message and believes in God who sent Me has eternal life, and will never be damned for his sins, but has already passed out of death into life" (John 5:24, LB).

From the very beginning, acceptance of life after death was the prominent part of every Christian sermon. (See Acts 4:33). You have the freedom to toss out all of Christianity, but if you hold on to any of its doctrines, you must also grapple with the claim of life after death.

IF THERE IS LIFE AFTER DEATH, WHO EXPERIENCES IT?

Everyone.

But before a complacency sets in with that news, realize that Jesus informs us that some will experience eternal rewards, and other eternal punishment (Matthew 25:46, John 5:29).

This life and the life to come are not two cycles independent of each other. What you do in this phase of existence directs your condition in the next.

Throughout the Bible God is portrayed as controlled by love, mercy, and justice. No one received from Him less than they deserve. His deep love for all mankind is proven by the fact that He sent His Son to take our punishment.

> For God loved the world so much that He gave His only Son so that anyone who believes in Him shall not perish but have eternal life (John 3:16).

No one will be able to honestly say, "God, it's not fair!"

He has assured us that

> "He has given us eternal life, and this life is in His Son. So whoever has God's Son has life; whoever does not have His Son, does not have life. I have written this to you who believe in the Son of God so that you may know you have eternal life (1 John 5:11-13).

WHAT ABOUT THE FATE OF UNBELIEVERS?

Jesus states clearly:

> And all who trust him ... God's Son ... to save them have eternal life; those who don't believe and obey Him shall never see heaven, but the wrath of God remains upon them (John 3:36, LB).

Hell is a biblical concept you can't ignore. You can laugh at it, scoff, or wish it out of existence. But, if it exists ... your attempts are futile.

I took my car to the mechanic. The verdict? I would need $750 to repair the transmission. I didn't want to hear that news. I tried to convince myself that it wasn't true. But, the truth couldn't be altered. The car wouldn't run until it was fixed.

"I don't want to hear about hell," many say.

Neither do I. But, it's better to know the score now than later, which may be too late.

WHAT HAPPENS WHEN BABIES DIE?

That's a good question. Also, how about the severely mentally retarded or others incapable of understanding? The Bible doesn't explain everything on this issue, but here's some of what it does say.

First, when mothers attempted to bring their little ones to Jesus, the disciples tried to chase them off. They assumed the children couldn't comprehend Jesus' words, would get in the way, and waste their master's valuable time. Jesus reprimands them.

> But when Jesus saw what was happening he was very much displeased with his disciples and said to them, "Let the children come to me for the Kingdom of God belongs to such as they. Don't send them away! I tell you as seriously as I know how that anyone who refuses to come to God as a little child will never be allowed into His Kingdom." Then He took the children into His arms and placed His hands on their heads and He blessed them (Mark 10:14-16).

Then, Israel's great King David gives us a clue about the destiny of little ones. David's faith is well documented. He is one whom God found to be "a man after His own heart" (1 Samuel 13:14, Acts 13:22). David agonized throughout the illness and death of his infant son. When he received the news of the baby's death he says, "I shall go to him, but he will not return to me" (1 Samuel 12:23).

The eternal destiny of both David and the baby would be the same.

WHAT WILL HEAVEN BE LIKE?

The Bible says that when Christ returns the believers in heaven and those on their way will reunite body and spirit (see 1 Corinthians 15:51-58; 1 Thessalonians 4:15-18). This uniting will produce a new body just like Jesus had after His resurrection (Philippians 3:21, 1 John 3:2). These bodies will be trans-spatial, that is, able to transport immediately to long distances and enter through solid objects (see John 20:26). Yet, they still perform purely physical acts such as eating food (see Luke 24:36-43).

The Bible reveals other facts about heaven.

It's Jesus' home, and the home He's building for each believer will be custom designed (John 14:2-14).

We will see God face to face (Revelation 22:4 and 1 Corinthians 13:12).

WILL PEOPLE RECOGNIZE EACH OTHER IN HEAVEN?

People retain their identities in the life to come. There's no great fusion of souls into a pool of misty spirits. You will be you. In every glimpse of heaven the Bible gives to us, this proves to be true.

In Mark 9:4 Jesus actually talks with two citizens of heaven. Their names are well known: Moses and Elijah.

In the story of the rich man and Lazarus (Luke 19), Jesus illustrates the point that the two men kept their pre-death resemblances.

This chapter's coverage of death and afterlife may seem far removed from the other subjects covered in the book. However, I believe there is an important correlation. Quality living must include more than just material security and personal ease. Your soul and spirit must discover quality as well.

Fear of death robs many people of a quality life.

Jesus came in order that He "could deliver those who through fear of death have been living all their lives as slaves to constant dread" (Hebrews 2:15, LB).

Few people will openly admit their anxiety about death. We go to great lengths to avoid confronting this fact of life. It is equally true that we can merely exist without reaching for quality spiritual living.

CHAPTER 11
IS IT REALLY WORTH GETTING UP EARLY ON SUNDAYS?

Just for a moment, suppose you're working the counter at a fast food place. You've just finished a hectic holiday rush hour. You survived even though one of your co-workers failed to show. You're trying to reorganize the catsup and plastic straws for the next onslaught. With sweat on your brow and a tired sigh, you turn to greet another customer.

Nothing memorable about his looks, but when he speaks ... "I know everything you've ever done," he states in all sincerity.

"You what?"

"I know what you've done. I know about the $10 overcount you pocketed ... and about you and Denise driving out to Lakeshore Park last Saturday ... and I know that when you were six years old, you had a dog named Ralphine," he says matter-of-factly.

You recoil. Has the C.I.A. been tailing you for the past fifteen years? The stranger continues. "I know I look fairly young. However, I've always existed. In fact, I remember the days of Julius Caesar like they were yesterday." He reminisces. "It was cloudy and threatening rain as he crossed the Rubi ... "

"What are you saying? You always existed?" you

interrupt.

"Certainly. What else would you expect of the Savior of the world? You see, I have a mission in life: to help people find eternal life."

You glance at the man. You get the feeling that he believes what he is saying. A crowd gathers, and you realize you need to get back to work. Yet, you stand and stare.

"In fact," he persists in a calm, even tone, "I'm the only way to get to heaven. I know there are all sorts of people trying to tell you supposed spiritual secrets. But the truth is, they are all either deceived or deceivers. I'm the only way."

You consider reaching for the phone to call the police. But, you're startled into inaction by the words, "I once died, and then came back to life again, in order that you, too, will be able to live forever. You see, I died for your sins, not for mine. I've never done anything wrong."

The entire personnel staff, and the customers, squeeze close to this man as he makes his appeal. "What I want you to do is believe in me, and thereby show that you believe in God, my Father, who sent me. You'll show that you truly believe by obeying my word. If you want to follow me, you'll need to give up your attachment to all things."

At this point a couple of hecklers begin to jeer. The man calmly continues. With a sense of sadness he reports, "If you fail to believe me, your eternal future is, indeed, bleak."

"Are you talking about hell?" one lady blurts out.

"The man is a weirdo. He sounds like he thinks he's God," another retorts.

An old man chimes in. "Yeah, and nobody can see

God."

Several demand that he's thrown out, so they can order their dinner. In the midst of the confusion, a sobbing woman hysterically throws herself at the man's feet. Another fellow you recognize as a regular customer, drops to his knees in front of the man and cries out, "My Lord, and my God." The whole crowd unexpectedly seems captivated by the scene.

Now, you do reach for the phone.

Who do you call? The police? A psychiatrist? The county emergency team? Or, do you call Mom? Dad? Brother? A friend? Your spouse? A roommate? And tell them to hurry down here to meet a man who'll change their life?

Chances are, you call one of the first. The claims appear too ridiculous, too impossible to believe. There is no way anyone would believe him, unless he has some objective evidence to support his statements. Unless he could impel reasonable people to follow him. Unless the entire bag of things he said was completely true. What if it were all true?

Let's take a closer look.

All the claims made by the above fictional man in the fast food joint were made by Jesus some two thousand years ago. In the Bible's own words, here are the similar scenes.

"Go and get our husband," Jesus told her.

'But I'm not married," the woman replied.

"All too true!" Jesus said. "For you have had five husbands, and you aren't even married to the man you're living with now."

Then the woman left her waterpot beside the well and went back to the village and told everyone, "Come and meet a man who told me everything I ever did! Can this be the Messiah?" So the people came streaming from the village to see Him (John 4:16-18, 28-30, LB).

"Your father Abraham rejoiced to see My day. He knew I was coming and was glad."

The Jewish leaders: "You aren't even fifty years old—sure, You've seen Abraham!"

Jesus: "The absolute truth is that I was in existence before Abraham was ever born!"

At that point the Jewish leaders picked up stones to kill Him. But Jesus was hidden from them, and walked past them and left the temple (John 8:56-59, LB).

Then the High Priest asked Him, "Are you the Messiah, the Son of God?"

Jesus said, "I am, and you will see Me sitting at the right hand of God, and returning to earth in the clouds of heaven" (Mark 14:61, 62).

After Jesus was executed by the Romans, His followers gathered in a room. Luke records:

Jesus Himself was suddenly standing there among them, and greeted them. But the whole group was terribly frightened, thinking they were seeing a ghost!

"Why are you frightened?" He asked. "Why do you doubt that it is really I? Look at My hands! Look at My feet! You can see that it is I, Myself! Touch Me and make sure that I am not a ghost! For ghosts don't have bodies, as you see I do!" As He spoke, He held out his hands for them to see [the marks of the nails], and showed them [the wounds in] His feet (Luke 24:36-44, LB).

"You know where I am going and how to get there."

"No, we don't," Thomas said. "We haven't any idea where You are going, so how can we know the way?"

Jesus told him, "I am the Way—yes, and the Truth and the Life. No one can get to the Father except by means of Me" (John 14:4-6, LB).

"I have not been telling you My own ideas, but have spoken what the Father has taught Me. And He who sent Me is with Me—He has not deserted Me— for I always do those things that are pleasing to Him" (John 8:28, 29, LB).

Then He called His disciples and the crowds to come over and listen. "If any of you want to be My follower," He told them, "you must put aside your own pleasures and shoulder your cross, and follow Me closely. If you insist on saving your life, you will lose it. Only those who throw away their lives for My sake and for the sake of the Good News will ever know what it means to really live" (Mark 8:34, 35, LB).

And all who trust Him—God's Son—to save them have eternal life; those who don't believe and obey Him shall never see heaven, but the wrath of God remains upon them (John 3:36, LB).

Phillip said, "Sir, show us the Father and we will be satisfied."

Jesus replied, "Don't you even yet know who I am, Phillip, even after all this time I have been with you? Anyone who has seen Me has seen the Father! So why are you asking to see Him? Don't you believe

that I am in the Father and the Father is in Me?"
(John 14:8-10, LB).

John tells us that one of Jesus' followers was not present when the resurrected Christ appeared to the others. He did not believe their story.

Eight days later the disciples were together again, and this time Thomas was with them. The doors were locked; but suddenly, as before, Jesus was standing among them and greeting them.

Then He said to Thomas, "Put your finger into My hands. Put your hand into my side. Don't be faithless any longer. Believe!"

"My Lord and my God!" Thomas said.

Then Jesus told him, "You believe because you have seen Me. But blessed are those who haven't seen Me and believe anyway" (John 20:26-29, LB).

These are remarkable assertions by one who demanded humility in others. If all He said about Himself is true, then he certainly requires careful consideration. If He's the one who forgives sin, teaches truth, bestows eternal life, and judges the world (as He said of Himself), then He is not to be ignored.

If, on the other hand, His claims are untrue, well, He was either a great imposter who has perpetrated upon mankind the most horrendous lie ever conceived (that is, giving false hope of a life to come), or, He was Himself so deceived and crazy that He should have been put away for the good of society. In the final analysis, these are the only choices left. Either Jesus is Lord, Savior, God, or a deranged deceiver who has grossly perverted our world.

Some people talk about Jesus as the great example for mankind (and He is). They have called Him the ultimate expression of love (which is certainly true). They even classify Him as a great moral teacher and philosopher (no question of that). However, Jesus Himself will not let you stop with that. If He was wrong about who He was then He is not a great example, or teacher, or anything else. Every individual must decide, was Jesus looney, or Lord?

To determine which, you have to look at some evidence. Belief in Christ has never been unreasonable, though it is a step of faith. It must be a decision based on will. No one was ever forced to believe. It is not a blind step. There are good, solid reasons for believing Christ is exactly who He says He is.

As you seek a quality spiritual life, you will want to gather as much objective evidence as possible. The serious searcher will enjoy a book such as *Evidence That Demands A Verdict*, by Josh McDowell (Here's Life Publishers, 1972).

A good place to begin is to examine the resurrection of Jesus Christ. As mentioned in the last chapter, Jesus rising from the dead is the central foundation of Christian teaching.

The apostle Paul said "if being a Christian is of value to us only now in this life, we are the most miserable of creatures" (1 Corinthians 15:19, LB).

If the resurrection is not true, let us pack it all up and go home. If it is not true, let's forget religion, ignore our spiritual longings, and live only for today.

But, Paul continues, "The fact is Christ did actually rise from the dead" (verse 20).

How could Paul be so confident?

FIRST, THE BODY COULD NOT BE FOUND

All the Gospels (Matthew, Mark, Luke, and John)

record the fact that the ladies who went to the tomb of Jesus on the first Easter morning were surprised to find the tomb empty. Their initial shock and disbelief demonstrate that they expected something else. Even though Jesus repeatedly predicted His suffering, death and resurrection (Mark 8:31ff, Mark 9:30-32, and Mark 10:32-34), it was too incredible for them to understand, or dare to hope for. There is no doubt, the tomb was empty.

Upon the veracity of the resurrection as well as all he wrote, the author of the book of Luke states: "Several biographies of Christ have already been written using as their source material the reports circulating among us from the early disciples and other eyewitnesses. However, it occurred to me that it would be well to recheck all these accounts from the first to last and after thorough investigation to pass this summary on to you, to reassure you of the truth of all you were taught" (Luke 1:1-4).

Luke, a Greek physician, had no trouble believing in the resurrection, even though he was not one of the witnesses of it. How did he learn about it? Initially, from the preaching of the early apostles. The resurrection was the nucleus of every sermon. The first recorded message after Christ's resurrection, and departure into heaven, was given by Peter. "God raised Him up again, putting an end to the agony of death" (Acts 2:24).

"And with great power the apostles were giving witness to the resurrection of the Lord Jesus, and abundant grace was upon them all" (Acts 4:33).

But could there be another explanation for why the tomb was empty? Here are the most often proposed alternatives.

Matthew reports that "Mary Magdalene and the other Mary" arrived at the grave early that morning. Critics propose, what if Mary and Mary got a little confused, walked down the wrong path, discovered another empty tomb, and assumed Jesus had risen from the dead.

To hold to this theory, you must believe that women are by nature overemotional, scatterbrained, and easily misled. But both Marys had been right at the graveside, watching his burial (Matthew 27:61). Also, you must believe that the other disciples were just as flighty. John says that both he and Peter ran to the tomb to check out the women's story (John 20:3ff).

In addition, you must believe that the Marys expected Jesus to rise from the dead and therefore jumped easily to this conclusion. There is hard evidence to the contrary. The women carried spices that they had prepared for a dead body. Also, when Mary Magdalene returned to the site later, and met the resurrected Lord she didn't recognize Him at first, because she had no idea that He was alive. She questioned Him as to where the body had been taken (John 20:13).

To believe in the Muddle-Mary Theory is to exhibit sexist prejudice, ignore plain facts, and to think that a 2,000-year-old worldwide movement can all begin by a mixup in a graveyard.

IT-WAS-ONLY-A-FLESH-WOUND THEORY

B-grade westerns made this an attractive idea to modern skeptics. You know the scene—the hero is shot in the arm, left in the desert to die, but somehow, probably due to a faithful horse, he survives the heat, catches the villain, and an exciting cliff-hanger fistfight occurs. There is the hero throwing punches with an arm that only moments before was almost blown off his body by a Sharps buffalo rifle. After the fight the hero exclaims to the swooning young lady, "Shucks, Miss Dolly, it's only a flesh wound."

Only in celluloid, never in real life. Yet, some insist that the dark, damp cave revived Jesus. He leaped to His feet, flung aside a large stone (that the women together couldn't move), and was in such robust health that everyone thought He had risen from the dead. To hold to this theory is to misunderstand many things about the ancient world.

Jesus was scourged before He was executed (John 19:1). A scourging consisted of a beating on the back with a whip that had lead bits imbedded in its leather thongs. Forty lashes could kill a man. A scourging was thirty-nine lashes.

After dragging a huge, heavy wooden cross through the streets until He collapsed, with blood streaming down His head from the crown of thorns crushed there, Jesus was so pitiful to look at that witnesses were moved to tears (Luke 23:27). His feet and hands were nailed to the cross, and it was lifted and dropped into the ground. After His death, and before He was taken down, a Roman soldier drove a spear through His side and jerked it out. This gruesome picture points out how incredible the flesh wound theory is.

Also, to believe such a theory is to arrogantly assume that those primitive Romans knew nothing about death. They didn't know a living man from a dead body. But, I ask, how many people have you watched die? How many bodies have you hauled down from a cross? Seasoned Roman executioners knew more about death and dying than many of us ever want to know.

Who-Stole-The-Body Theory

Some wish to explain away the disappearing body by suggesting it was stolen. But, who did the stealing? There is no agreement by theorists on this point. Some say thieves. But, what for? There was no conceivable reason to carry off the broken, battered, naked body of a penniless prophet.

Some suppose it was the followers themselves. They took the body in order to perpetuate the resurrection hoax. This is the oldest theory. Matthew 28:13 reveals how the Jewish priests began that same rumor themselves. But, what motive would they have for such a concoction? It gained them neither money nor power. In fact, it brought them death. How easy it would have been when confronted with their own deaths, to expose the whole thing. Yet, not one witness of the resurrection ever recanted his position.

Others state that the Roman or Jewish authorities moved the body so it wouldn't become a shrine for religious zealots. This is absurd. Both causes had everything to gain by squelching this new movement as soon as possible. All they needed to do was exhibit the body. Neither Romans nor Jews ever produced the body of Jesus.

After two thousand years, no one has come close to disproving the resurrection of Jesus Christ.

But, that's just one part of the evidence. There's more.

SECOND, JESUS WAS SEEN ALIVE AFTER HIS DEATH

We want first-hand witnesses. That is what the Bible gives us. John, one of the apostles and witnesses, states: "Christ was alive when the world began, yet I myself have seen Him with my own eyes and listened to Him speak. I have touched Him with my own hands. He is God's message of Life" (1 John 1:1).

Of course, you can discount a witness's statement. The apostles may have invented the whole thing. But why?

Why die for something you made up? And, if they were inventions, they were poor ones. Wouldn't you have Him appear to more authoritative viewers? Wouldn't it have been better to tell a story that was exactly the same in all four Gospel accounts? Why make it complicated by trying to figure out the hour-by-hour happenings after the resurrection? Besides, if you're making up such a story, why conjecture such uncertainty, even doubt, in the minds of the apostles? That wouldn't help establish their early leadership.

Maybe the apostles were just seeing things: hallucinations. If we disregard the trivial speculation of spiked mushrooms, some say it was a wish fulfillment of hurting apostles. They just imagined it, because they wanted to see him so badly. But neither the environment (locked in a room, fearful of arrest by roman authorities) nor their dispositions (utter dejection due to their failed cause) support such conjecture. Besides, the sheer number of appearances, to a wide variety of people, make it sound as though hundreds of people had to live in a continual state of delusion.

He appeared to ...

Mary Magdalene, and the other Mary (Matthew 28:9), on their way back to the others. They greeted him with fear and awe.

The eleven apostles (Judas was no longer around) (Matthew 28:17) in Galilee. Some worshipped, some still had doubts.

To Mary Magdalene alone (Mark 16:9), when she returned to the grave later that day.

To the eleven, as they gathered in a building for dinner (Mark 16:14). They were reproached for not believing earlier witnesses.

To two followers on their way to Emmaus (Luke 24:31), who were puzzled over the recent events. They were slow to recognize the risen Lord.

To Peter (Luke 24:34).

Again, to the apostles, and other followers (Luke 24:36). They were doubting and troubled at the time. At the town of Bethany, outside Jerusalem (verse 50). They were filled with great joy, and returned to the temple to praise God.

To the ten (Thomas was gone) (John 20:19), where they huddled in fear of the Jewish authorities.

To the eleven, the following week (John 20:26), Thomas' doubts quickly vanished.

To seven of the disciples at the Sea of Galilee (John 21:1), where they had gone to resume their fishing careers.

To a non-believer, Saul, on the Damascus road (Acts 9:5).

To James (1 Corinthians 15:7).

And to more than 500 believers at one time (1 Cor. 15:6).

How many more witnesses are needed? Volumes of history have been written on far less.

THIRD, PEOPLE'S LIVES CHANGED

The apostles were changed men. They had denied Christ, fled when He was arrested, and hid in a locked room. A few days later they threw open the doors with much confidence and sacrificial zeal and threw themselves with fearless abandon into their message.

What changed Peter from coward to chief preacher in the Jerusalem church? What occurred to make James, Jesus' half-brother, leader of the early church, instead of a doubter? And what about Paul? He stopped arresting and torturing Christians in order to become their leading spokesman. What happened: The Bible explains simply, they saw the risen Lord.

The evidence for the resurrection mounts.

John Stott quotes Sir Edward Clarke:

"As a lawyer I have made a prolonged study of the evidences for the events of the first Easter Day. To me the evidence is conclusive, and over and over again in the High Court I have secured the verdict on evidence not nearly so compelling. Inference follows on evidence, and a truthful witness is always artless and disdains effect. The Gospel evidence for the resurrection is of this class, and as a lawyer I accept it unreservedly as the testimony of truthful men to facts they were able to substantiate" John Stott, *Basic Christianity*, Downers Grove, Illinois, Inter-Varsity Press, 1958, page 47).

There is similar support for all Christian beliefs. You can use your whole mind and examine the claims. Think it through. Ponder the commands. Discuss the implications. But faith requires a decisive step. As in every other aspect of quality living, becoming a Christian involves an active decision of the will.

Here are some suggestions:

1. Look for yourself. Investigate. Read the Gospel of Mark (it takes less than two hours), or other Bible passages. I've been quoting from the *Living Bible.* If you've never read much in the Bible before, try this version.

Look at some good books on Christian basics, such as *More Than A Carpenter,* Josh McDowell; *Basic Christianity,* John Stott; *Mere Christianity,* C.W. Lewis; or *Knowing God,* J.I. Packer (see bibliography).

Talk to people that you trust, people who have a personal, vital relationship with Jesus Christ.

2. Consider your own needs. Has a lack of spiritual commitment gnawed at you since childhood? Do you still have an emptiness regardless of other elements of quality living? Do you sense that you've missed something?

For you, it might be the mounting evidence that draws you to make your conclusion. Or, it could be an overwhelming sense of God's love and care for you. It takes someone who can set other pressure aside to say, "I need to do this for myself."

3. Discover what God has done. Make sure you understand the basics. Things like:

God desires you to live satisfying, meaningful life right now, and enjoy eternity with Him.

Disobedience and rebellion of the human race has perverted God's world. If you ignore God you are outside His family.

God made a provision for you to return to fellowship with Him. He sent His son, Jesus Christ, to die for your sins. God's plan is just, and brilliant.

Acceptance of Jesus Christ is the only way you can establish a quality spiritual relationship with God. No one is pure enough on his own to get to heaven. You must receive God's free gift of salvation.

4. Decide. You have to make up your mind. Go for it, don't hold back. Talk to God. Tell Him you're ready to face up to who you really are. Ask forgiveness for your disobedience. Tell Him that you really do believe Jesus is all He says He is. Ask Him to come into your life and take control of it. Jesus says in Revelation 3:20, "Look, I have been standing at the door and am constantly knocking. If anyone hears me calling him and opens the door, I will come in and fellowship with him and he with me" (LB). By faith, accept the fact that He has and learn to know His presence.

5. Follow through. Join a fellowship of believers. Schedule a regular time of talking to God. Commit yourself to reading through the whole Bible. Make your commitment public. Tell other people. Get involved with a study group where you have the freedom to ask questions and discover answers. Attend a church regularly. Don't stop with the minimum. Explore, grow, accept changes as you follow God's leading. Take up some studies in deeper Christian growth like my book, *Radical Discipleship.*

No matter how much quality you discover in all the other areas of your life, you will always want more. Your spirit will cry out for recognition and fulfillment. Don't stop one step short of a quality spiritual life.

CHAPTER 12
COME ON ALONG!

Dusty Jack Scarborough still climbs the little Salmon Gulch. This is his 63rd year of doing so. Somewhere up the creek and to the right he expects to find it—the mother lode—veins of gold so thick he dreams about them most every night.

Chuck and Cherie Osborn live in Triple Creek, Oregon. You'll never find it on a map. They hope you'll never find it—period! Fleeing from the doom they're confident will come upon America's cities, they hibernate in a remote part of Oregon's eastern plains. With food, water and ammunition, they expect to be some of the few survivors of the upcoming nuclear holocaust.

A one-room flop on Selma Street isn't Maggie's idea of a grand Hollywood reception. She came from England to be a star. She's a waitress at the Glamorous Gown All-Night Cafeteria.

Everybody's seeking something.

Money. Security. Fame.

What are you seeking?

Some never find what they seek. They're the more fortunate. Nothing's sadder than finding what you seek and facing the disappointment. Usually, what you have reached is not worth the difficult journey it took to get you there.

I know that one of the things you're seeking is quality living in a complicated age. This book is full of hints about the possibilities. Total quality won't be achieved, however, until you spend some time seeking Jesus Christ. I want to make sure you don't miss Him.

John the Baptist had some friends who were seekers. They had followed John's ministry. They saw him stand in the Jordan River and baptize folks for the forgiveness of their sins. They also heard John say that he was not the Messiah. So, they waited.

One day it happened.

One day the Savior of the world walked their way. The wait proved worthwhile.

"Behold!" John announced, "The Lamb of God who takes away the sins of the world!" (John 1:29).

They needed no other prompting. They immediately followed after this one John proclaimed. When Jesus saw them tagging along, He turned and quizzed them, "What do you seek?"

WHAT DO YOU SEEK?

It's a good question.

During the last few chapters you've taken a quick look at Jesus. Now, He's turned around to look you in the eye, and asks, "What do you seek?"

This may be catching you off guard. That's the way I felt when He asked me the same thing. It wasn't the discourse I expected at all.

I wouldn't have been surprised if He'd said, "Have you finally come to this? Well, Steve, old boy, I've been waiting for you for a long time. After all, you're such an intelligent, wise chap. It's good to have you aboard. We can use folks like you on the team. Yes, you've made the right choice."

Or something like that.

But He didn't.

Other times I feared He might ask, "Did you get yourself straightened out yet? Here you're sniveling after Me and you haven't got the foggiest idea what you should be doing. There's selfishness and other sludge down inside you. You don't expect Me to accept something as grimy as that, do you? Get your act together before you come dogging after Me."

Sometimes I thought He'd say that.

But He didn't.

"What do you seek?"

That's always His first question ... to you, me, everyone. Let me give you the 10 most often used wrong answers, and then you'll understand the importance of the only correct one.

"What do you seek?"

"I want to get out of this jam. I've had a sudden reversal of fortunes. Why, at this time last year everything was smooth sailing. I had a great job. I had so much money I didn't know what to do with it all. That's when I got into silver. Bought pounds of coins. Then, the bottom dropped out, and I took a terrible loss. Had to take a weekend job, sell my car, get a loan from my Dad.

"Then I read this fantastic story about a fellow in Tulsa who was in worse shape than me. He got religion and the whole mess was straightened out. Got himself the biggest Cadillac dealership in the state. So, I figured You could do the same for me ... "

"What do you seek?"

"I want to achieve my goal. All my life I've been

fat. It's all my mother's fault. She fed me too much when I was young. Anyway, I've tried every diet known to mankind. The Grapefruit Diet, the 1000-Calorie Diet, Dr. Whamo's Miracle Diet, the Cream Puff Diet, and even the Oriental Diet of Extreme Displeasure. I've used pills, liquids, swallowed bran, and even tried being a breath-a-terian.

"Then, I saw Sally Stanworthy at the class reunion. She'd lost thirty pounds since high school. 'Sally,' I said, 'you must tell me your secret.' She told me, 'It was only with the Lord's help.' I said to myself right then, if Sally can lose thirty pounds, I should be able to lose forty.' So, here I am."

There you are.

"What do you seek?"

"I figure it doesn't hurt to cover all the bases. I've always been a cautious person. I brush my teeth after every meal. Darn the holes in my socks. Only cross streets at crosswalks. The minute I feel a cold coming on, I take lots of Vitamin C, drink liquids, and get plenty of rest. I've got comprehensive health insurance, dental insurance, car insurance, life insurance, fire insurance, home insurance, spouse insurance, and even feline insurance (on Fluffy).

"The way I figure it, a person can't be too careful. That's why I heard about the possiblity that some folks might be headed to a place that wasn't too... er, cool. After all, isn't that your business?"

Not entirely.

"What do you seek?"

"I was just wondering what all the excitement's about. I really hadn't given it much thought. But last Thursday I was playing racquetball with Hap Stevens. He told me all about this great Bible study he attended. Well, Hap's always been a little weird. But then, Curt Benson began singing some song about Jesus while we waited for a court. And Curt is club president this year. If I ever expect to get anywhere, I'd better start sending money to Billy Graham or something. Know what I mean?"

Yes, I'm afraid I do.

"What do you seek?"

"I need a little peace with my in-laws. I'm getting married in June, and my fiancee's family are church-going folks. They seem to like me, but they keep saying they hope Cheryl's marrying a Christian. Now, I really do love Cheryl and I've always said I'd do anything for her. I'd better put up or shut up. What the heck, church can't be all that bad. Until football season, that is. So I'm going to be a good sport."

Nice try.

"What do you seek?"

"I'll be right up front with You. I'm hoping for a free lunch. I'm no phony, I'm looking for the old gravy train. If all I've heard about You is true, then You can calm storms, raise the dead, turn water into wine, and feed the multitudes. That's for me. Psychic power. Miracles. I want to be plugged in to all the riches of God. I want all the physical and spiritual goodies, pure and simple."

It's simple, but not pure.

"What do you seek?"

"What I really need is to broaden my power base. I've given my life to social causes. I always try to look out for others. Active in charities, elected to the school board when I was only twenty-three. Now I have an opportunity to be of real service to my fellow man. The party asked me to consider running for

Congress. I'm no novice who was born yesterday. It'll take some campaign to unseat old Frankley. He'll line up the unions, and I think I can build rapport up on the Heights. But, what about the "born again" crowd? They're a force to be reckoned with.

"I figured if I had a mild bout with religion, that would satisfy them. At least, it would look good in print. Don't get me wrong. I'm not saying I'm going to fake it. That's not my style. I honestly want the real thing, I just don't want to overdo it."

Don't worry, you won't.

"What do you seek?"

"I had in mind an expansion of my metaphysical knowledge. I believe that too many modern minds are dwarfed by lack of consideration of the spiritual dimension of life. They fall into the trap of relying solely on the senses. That's foolish. We overlook the entire history of the human race and its constant quest for the spirit world. Whether or not there's any reality, I won't know until I explore. I intend to pursue every avenue, and collect all the knowledge I can. That's being open-minded. That's what education's all about."

Is it?

"What do you seek?"

"It's hard to explain. What I really want is sort of, you know ... a tingly religious feeling. I saw this girl on T.V. She explained that when she became a Christian a flood of emotions swept through her. She thought she was lifted right off the ground. Then she saw a giant cross hovering over her. For days after, she felt an overwhelming love for everyone she met. That's the kind of thing I want. Can You imagine such a neat experience? I can hardly wait for what will happen next?"

Yawn.

"What do you seek?"

"That's easy. I want no more pain. A few years ago six hundred pounds of lumber mill equipment crushed my right knee. The doctor said I would either lose the leg, or have to put up with the pain the rest of my life. I chose pain, but sometimes, I wonder if I did the right thing. I've heard You can heal. I believe it. I don't see why it shouldn't happen to me. Nobody should have to put up with what I do. Healing's the least You could do for me."

Why settle for the least?

"What do you seek?"

Jesus still asks. Perhaps you wouldn't answer like any of the above. Few folks are so blatant. I just eliminated some of the fluff and finesse. You need to do the same with your reasons. Dig down deep. Why is it you want to know God? Weigh your motives. Not much point in kidding yourself.

Okay, maybe you're wondering, what is the acceptable reason for seeking Jesus? It's right there in John 1:38. The disciples said, "Teacher, where are You staying?" They implied, "Jesus, we just want to be where You are."

No demands.

No conditions.

No hesitations.

We want to be with You.

Sounds simple, but it isn't.

You don't know where Jesus will lead you. You have no idea what that means for your future. It might be to a palace, or on the other hand, it might be to a dungeon. It might mean victories, or constant battles. You may be all alone with Him, or maybe in a crowd of millions.

"What are you seeking?"

Jesus, I want to be where You are.

I hope you won't have the problem many do at this point. You come this far, pledge yourself to follow Jesus, and immediately allow something to interfere. Mary didn't let that happen.

Mary and her sister, Martha, invited Jesus to their house. While Martha slaved away in the kitchen, cooking for the crew, Mary sat at Jesus' feet to listen to His every word. This provoked Martha. She needed help. When she complained, Jesus replied, "Martha, Martha, you are worried and bothered about so many things; but only a few things are necessary, really only one, for Mary has chosen the good part, which shall not be taken away from her" (Luke 10:41).

I want to be with Jesus, Mary said with her single-minded action.

The crowd told him to be quiet. He was making a fool of himself. Blind Bartimaeus wasn't about to shut up. "Jesus, son of David! Have mercy on me!" he yelled.

Jesus called back, "Hurry up, and come here." Bartimaeus didn't hesitate.

Can you imagine a blind man jumping up and running through a crowd? How many times did he stumble, or fall? Yet, he rushed on. He wanted to be with Jesus.

"Oh," you say, "he just wanted to be healed."

Not so. Jesus did heal him, but when Jesus said, "Go your way," Bartimaeus wouldn't leave. He followed the path to Jerusalem with the soon-to-be-crucified Jesus.

Peter and Andrew had a nice little fishing business in the Sea of Galilee. Nothing fancy, just an honest, respectable business. Oh, it was hard work. Boats to repair, nets to mend, long hours ... Then, this Jesus walked along the shore one day, and looked them in the eye. "Come on along," he said.

They went.

No goodbyes. No selling the business. No months of meditation. They just left. They wanted to be with Jesus.

Dwarfish little Zaccheus was the most talked about person in Jericho, the prime butt of most of the jokes. He was also the richest man in town. Chief Tax Collector was his title, but Chief Thief was his popular label. Not a very likely candidate for a smashing spiritual awakening.

He was so short he couldn't see over people's heads. But, he wanted a glimpse of Jesus. It was a cinch no one would make room for him. So, up the tree he climbed, out on a literal limb to see this man from Galilee. What snickers would circulate in the streets tonight, but he didn't care. He wanted to get to where Jesus was.

He made it.

What about those disciples of John the Baptist mentioned earlier? How did Jesus respond to their right answer? He said, "Come and see." Come on along, fellows.

Come on along.

That's what Jesus has been saying for thousands of years.

Come along, Mary.

Come on along, Bartimaeus.

Come on along, Peter and Andrew.

Come on along, Zaccheus.

Come on along, Steve.

Come on along.

There's a sense in which this is the end of the trail for you and me. We've been on an uphill climb. But now, we've come to the really hard part ... finding a quality spiritual life. You've been introduced to Jesus Christ. Now He beckons to both of us to hurry on toward His unique expression of total quality living.

The Christian is ultimately called on to serve, to pick up his cross daily (Luke 9:23), and to give sacrificially of himself (Matthew 25:31-46 and James 1:27 for instance). The scope of this book does not cover this, but quality living does not mean standing still. As you follow Jesus, you will find within yourself a deep desire to grow in these areas. And as you grow, you will be expressing His definition of quality living.

I wouldn't miss it for the world.

I'm going.

You can spend your days in the souvenir shop of life, dallying with the trinkets and trivia. Or you can leave the crowd and head further up the trail.

There will be dangers. Steep grades to climb. Treacherous canyons to cross. Sometimes violent storms. Ah, but there'll be sights you never dreamed existed. Views—of this world and the one to come— that will take your breath away. That's quality living ... peaceful satisfaction, freedom from guilt, and clean, refreshing tastes of eternity.

But He's heading on out, and He won't wait forever.

Come on along, and find out what true quality living is all about.

COME ON ALONG!
Let's do it.

REFERENCES

Adams, Douglas—*The Hitchhiker's Guide to the Galaxy,* New York: Harmony Books, 1979.

Adams, Douglas—*The Restaurant at the End of the Universe,* New York: Harmony Books, 1980.

Adams, Douglas—*Life, the Universe and Everything,* New York: Harmony Books, 1982.

Bly, Stephen A.—*Radical Discipleship,* Chicago, Illinois: Moody Press, 1981.

Bly, Stephen A.—*God's Angry Side,* Chicago, Illinois: Moody Press, 1982.

Bright, Bill—*The Holy Spirit: Key To Supernatural Living,* San Bernardino, California: Here's Life Publishers, Inc., 1980.

Brownstone, David M., and Hawes, Gene R.—*The Complete Career Guide,* New York: Simon & Schuster, 1980.

Douglass, Stephen B.—*Managing Yourself,* San Bernardino, California: Here's Life Publishers, Inc., 1978.

Douglass, Stephen B. and Lee Roddy—*Making The Most Of Your Mind,* San Bernardino, California: Here's Life Publishers, Inc., 1983.

Hoyt, Wade E., et al.—*Reader's Digest Complete Car Care Manual,* Pleasantville, New York: The Reader's Digest Association, Inc., 1981.

Lewis, C.S.—*Mere Christianity,* New York: The Macmillan Company, 1943.

McDowell, Josh—*Evidence That Demands A Verdict.* San Bernardino, California: Here's Life Publishers, Inc., 1972.

McDowell, Josh—*Reasons Skeptics Should Consider Christianity,* San Bernardino, California: Here's Life Publishers, Inc., 1981.

Packer, J.I.—*Knowing God,* Downers Grove, Illinois: Inter-Varsity Press, 1973.

Reuben, David, M.D.—*Everything You Always Wanted To Know About Nutrition,* New York: Simon & Schuster, 1978.

Rohrer, Virginia and Norman—*How To Eat Right And Feel Great,* Wheaton, Illinois: Tyndale Publishing House, 1977.

Stott, John R.W.—*Basic Christianity,* Downers Grove, Illinois: Inter-Varsity Press, 1958.

Solzhenitsyn, Aleksandr Isaevich; Thomas B. Whitney, trans.— *First Circle,* New York: Harper and Row, 1968.

Toffler, Alvin—*The Third Wave,* New York: William Morrow and Company, Inc., 1980.

Veninga, Robert L. Ph.D. and Spradley, James P., Ph.D.—The Work Stress Connection, Boston: Little, Brown and Company, 1981.